# SQL

## The Practical Beginner's Guide to Learn SQL Programming in One Day Step-by-Step (#2020 Updated Version | Effective Computer Programming)

### Steve Tudor

**Text Copyright**

All rights reserved. No part of this guide may be reproduced in any form without permission in writing from the publisher except in the case of brief quotations embodied in critical articles or reviews.

**Legal & Disclaimer**

The information contained in this book and its contents is not designed to replace or take the place of any form of medical or professional advice; and is not meant to replace the need for independent medical, financial, legal or other professional advice or services, as may be required. The content and information in this book has been provided for educational and entertainment purposes only.

The content and information contained in this book has been compiled from sources deemed reliable, and it is accurate to the best of the Author's knowledge, information and belief. However, the Author cannot guarantee its accuracy and validity and cannot be held liable for any errors and/or omissions. Further, changes are periodically made to this book as and when needed. Where appropriate and/or necessary, you must consult a professional (including but not limited to your doctor, attorney, financial advisor or such other professional advisor) before using any of the suggested remedies, techniques, or information in this book.

Upon using the contents and information contained in this book, you agree to hold harmless the Author from and against any damages, costs, and expenses, including any legal fees potentially resulting from the application of any of the information provided by this book. This disclaimer applies to any loss, damages or injury caused by the use and application, whether directly or indirectly, of any advice or information presented, whether for breach of contract, tort, negligence, personal injury, criminal intent, or under any other cause of action.

You agree to accept all risks of using the information presented inside this book.

You agree that by continuing to read this book, where appropriate and/or necessary, you shall consult a professional (including but not limited to your doctor, attorney, or financial advisor or such other advisor as needed) before using any of the suggested remedies, techniques, or information in this book.

# Table of Contents

**Chapter 1. INTRODUCTION** ................................................................. 9

    a. Introduction to SQL ................................................................ 10

    b. how to start coding ................................................................ 16

        Data Definition Language ................................................... 16

        Data Query Language ........................................................ 17

        Data Control Language ...................................................... 17

        Data Administration Commands ....................................... 18

        Transactional Control Commands ..................................... 18

    c. how to install MySQL applications .................................... 20

    d. how to launch MySQL Workbench ................................... 21

    e. Writing the first MySQL code. .......................................... 23

**Chapter 2. DATABASE** ........................................................................ 25

    a. How to create a SQL database ........................................... 25

    b. how to use a database ......................................................... 32

    c. how to delete a database .................................................... 33

    d. how to administrate the database ...................................... 33

**Chapter 3. TABLES** ............................................................................. 35

    Create tables ............................................................................ 35

    Deleting Tables ....................................................................... 39

    Inserting Data into a Table ..................................................... 42

    Dropping a Table .................................................................... 45

Using the ALTER TABLE Query .................................................. 46

**Chapter 4. DATA ............................................................. 52**

    Constraints in MySQL ............................................................ 53

    Updating Data .......................................................................... 54

    Pivoting Data ............................................................................ 60

    Deleting data ............................................................................ 62

**Chapter 5. SELECTING DATA ...................................... 64**

    Selecting rows and columns ................................................... 64

    Filtering rows and columns .................................................... 67

    Updating Data .......................................................................... 70

    Creating Indexes ...................................................................... 75

    Functions .................................................................................. 76

    MySQL Functions .................................................................... 76

    Joins .......................................................................................... 79

    Union ........................................................................................ 81

    ALIASES .................................................................................. 81

**Chapter 6. VIEWS ............................................................ 83**

**Chapter 7. What is a view, how to create a view, how to alter a view, deleting a view ........................................................ 86**

**Chapter 8. TRIGGERS .................................................... 92**

**Chapter 9. VARIABLES AND STORED ROUTINES ........... 94**

    Variables .................................................................................. 94

    Stored routines ........................................................................ 98

    Stored procedures ................................................................. 105

    Stored functions ................................................................ 114

    Deleting stored routines ..................................................... 119

**Chapter 10. CONTROL FLOW TOOLS ................................... 128**

    IF statement..................................................................... 128

    CASE statement ............................................................... 129

    WHILE statement ............................................................ 130

    LOOP statement............................................................... 131

**Chapter 11. CURSORS ............................................................ 133**

**Chapter 12. Common beginner mistakes and how to fix them 135**

**Chapter 13. Tips and tricks of SQL ........................................ 138**

    Four Tips That Make Using SQL Easier! ....................... 141

**Chapter 14. Workbook ............................................................ 143**

    What is the schema?........................................................ 143

    How to create a new table .............................................. 145

    How to create a table with one that already exists ........ 145

    How to drop tables ......................................................... 146

    How to Do Your Own Search Results Through SQL .... 148

        How to create a new query..................................... 148

        How to work with the SELECT command ............ 149

        How does case sensitivity work? ........................... 151

**Chapter 15. SQL Quiz ............................................................. 155**

**CONCLUSION........................................................................ 157**

# Chapter 1. INTRODUCTION

If you are interested in learning a new coding language, there are a lot of different options that you can choose from, and it really depends on what you are looking for and what you want to do with them. Some of these languages are good for helping you to create a good website. Some are good for creating a smartphone application or for working on your own game to share with others. And then you can also choose a coding language that is like SQL, which are meant to help businesses stay organized and keep track of their information without all the challenges that can come with this.

Traditionally, many companies would choose to work with the 'Database Management System,' or the DBMS to help them to keep organized and to keep track of their customers and their products. This was the first option that was on the market for this kind of organization, and it does work well. Some newer methods that have changed the way that companies can sort and hold their information. Even when it comes to the most basic management system for data that you can choose, you will see that there is a ton more power and security than you would have found in the past.

Big companies will be responsible for holding onto a lot of data, and some of this data will include personal information about their customers like address, names, and credit card information. Because of the more complex sort of information that these businesses need to store, a new 'Relational Database Management System' has been created to help keep this information safe in a way that the DBMS has not been able to.

Now, as a business owner, there are some different options that you can pick from when you want to get a good database management system. Most business owners like to go with SQL because it is one of the best options out there. The SQL language is easy to use, was designed to work well with businesses, and it will give you all the tools that you need to make sure that your information is safe. Let's take some more time to look at this SQL and learn how to make it work for your business.

### a. Introduction to SQL

It is best to start at the beginning. SQL is a programming language that stands for 'Structured Query Language,' and it is a simple language to learn considering it will allow interaction to occur between the different databases that are in the same system. This database system first came out in the 70s, but when IBM came out with its own prototype of this programming language, then it really started to see a growth in popularity and the business world started to take notice.

The version of SQL that was originally used by IBM, known back then as ORACLE, was so successful that the team behind it eventually left IBM and became its own company. ORACLE, thanks to how it can work with SQL, is still one of the leaders in programming languages and it is always changing so that it can keep up with everything that is needed in the programming and database management world.

The SQL is a set of instructions that you can use to interact with your relational database. While there are a lot of languages that you can use to do this, SQL is the only language that most databases can understand. Whenever you are ready to interact with one of these databases, the software can go in and translate the commands that you are given, whether you are giving them in form entries or mouse clicks. These will be translated into SQL statements that the database will already be able to interpret.

If you have ever worked with a software program that is database driven, then it is likely that you have used some form of SQL in the past. It is likely that you didn't even know that you were doing this though. For example, there are a lot of dynamic web pages that are database driven. These will take some user input from the forms and clicks that you are making and then will use this information to compose a SQL query. This query will then go through and retrieve the information from the database to perform the action, such as switch over to a new page.

To illustrate how this works, think about a simple online catalog that allows you to search. The search page will often contain a form that will just have a text box. You can enter the name of the item that you would like to search using the form and then you would simply need to click on the search button. As soon as you click on the search button, the web server will go through and search through the database to find anything related to that search term. It will bring those back to create a new web page that will go along with your specific request.

For those who have not spent that much time at all learning a programming language and who would not consider themselves programmers, the commands that you would use in SQL are not too hard to learn. Commands in SQL are all designed with a syntax that fits in with the English language.

At first, this will seem really complicated, and you may be worried about how much work it will be to get it set up. But when you start to work on a few codes, you will find that it is not actually that hard to work with. Often, just reading out the SQL statement will help you to figure out what the command will do. Take a look at the code below:

**How this works with your database**

If you decide that SQL is the language that you will work on for managing your database, you can take a look at the database. You will notice that when you look at this, you are basically just looking at groups of information. Some people will consider these to be organizational mechanisms that will be used to store information that you, as the user, can look at later on, and it can do this as effectively as possible. There are a ton of things that SQL can help you with when it comes to managing your database, and you will see some great results.

There are times when you are working on a project with your company, and you may be working with some kind of database that is very similar to SQL, and you may not even realize that you are doing this. For example, one database that you commonly use is the phone book. This will contain a ton of information about people in your area including their name, what business they are in, their address, and their phone numbers. And all this information is found in one place so you won't have to search all over to find it.

This is kind of how the SQL database works as well. It will do this by looking through the information that you have available through your company database. It will sort through that information so that you are better able to find what you need the most without making a mess or wasting time.

**Client and server technology**

In the past, if you were working with a computer for your business, you were most likely using a mainframe computer. What this means is that the machines were able to hold onto a large system, and this system would be good at storing all the information that you need and for processing options. The user would be able to get onto these computers and interact with the mainframe, which in this case would be a 'dumb' terminal or one that is not able to interact all on its own. To get the information to show up the correct function, the dumb terminal would need to rely on all the information that is inside the computer, such as the memory, processor, and storage.

Now, these systems were able to work, and they got the job done for a very long time. If your company uses these and this is what you are most comfortable with using, it does get the work done. But there are some options on the market that will do a better job. These options can be found in the client-server system.

These systems will use some different processes to help you to get the results that are needed. With this one, the main computer that you are using, which would be called the 'server,' will be accessible to any user who is on the network. Now, these users must have the right credentials to do this, which helps to keep the system safe and secure. But if the user has the right information and is on your network, they can reach the information without a lot of trouble and barely any effort. The user can get the server from other servers or from their desktop computer, and the user will then be known as the 'client' so that the client and server are easily able to interact through this database.

**How to work with databases that are online**

There are a lot of business owners who will find that the client and server technology is the one that works for them. This system is great for many companies, but there are some things that you will need to add or take away at times because of how technology has been changing lately. There are some companies that like the idea that their database will do better with the internet so that they can work on this database anywhere they are located, whether they are at home or at the office. There are even times when a customer will have an account with the company, and they will need to be able to access the database online as well. For example, if you have an account with Amazon, you are a part of their database, and you can gain access to certain parts through this.

As the trend continues for companies to move online, it is more common to see that databases are moving online as well and that you must have a website and a good web browser so that the customer can come in and check them out. You can always add in usernames and passwords to make it more secure and to ensure that only the right user can gain access to their information. This is a great idea to help protect personal and payment information of your customers. Most companies will require that their users pick out security credentials to get on the account, but they will offer the account for free.

Of course, this is a system that is pretty easy to work with, but there will be a number of things going on behind the scenes to make sure that the program will work properly. The customer can simply go onto the system and check the information with ease, but there will be a lot of work for the server to do to make sure that the information is showing up on the screen in the right way, and to ensure that the user will have a good experience and actually see their own account information on the screen.

For example, you may be able to see that the web browser that you are using uses SQL or a program that is similar to it, to figure out the user that your data is hoping to see. The SQL system will be used to reach your database, as soon as the customer can put in what they are looking for. The SQL system, will see this query. And then bring back information on the website that will show up on the web browser, and if the system is working properly, the right information will show up on the page.

**Why is SQL so great?**

The various types of database management systems that you can work with, it is time to discuss why you would want to choose SQL over some of the other options that are out there. You not only have the option of working with other databases but also with other coding languages, and there are benefits to choosing each one. So, why would you want to work with SQL in particular? Some of the great benefits that you can get from using SQL as your database management system includes:

**Incredibly fast**

If you would like to pick out a management system that can sort through the information quickly and will get the results back in no time, then SQL is one of the best programs to use for this. You will be surprised at how much information you can get back, and how quickly it will come back to you. In fact, out of all the options, this is the most efficient one that you can go with.

**Well defined standards**

The database that comes with SQL is one that has been working well for a long time. In addition, it has been able to develop some good standards that ensure the database is strong and works the way that you want. Some of the other databases that you may want to work with will miss out on these standards, and this can be frustrating when you use them.

**You do not need a lot of coding**

If you are looking into the SQL database, you do not need to be an expert in coding to get the work done. We will take a look at a few codes that can help, but even a beginner will get these down and do well when working in SQL.

**Keeps your stuff organized**

When it comes to running your business, it is important that you can keep your information safe and secure as well as organized. And while there are a ton of great databases that you can go with, none will work as well as the SQL language at getting this all done.

Object-**oriented** DBMS

The database of SQL relies on the DBMS system that we talked about earlier because this will make it easier to find the information that you are searching for, to store the right items, and do so much more within the database.

The benefits that you can get when you choose to work with the SQL program. While some people do struggle with this interface in the beginning, but overall there are a ton of good features to work on with SQL, and you will really enjoy how fast and easy it is to work with this language and its database.

### b. how to start coding

SQL is easy to learn, and you won't have a lot of different commands in order to bring up the information that you want. In this chapter, we are going to spend some time learning some of these commands as well as separating the commands into the six different categories that are the best for them. These six categories include:

### Data Definition Language

This one is also known as the DDL, and it is one of the aspects that is inside of your SQL program that is in charge of allowing you to generate objects into the database before arranging them the way that you enjoy the best. For example, this is the aspect of the system that you will use when you would like to make changes, such as adding or deleting objects, out of the table. The commands that you would be able to use for this including:

- Drop index
- Drop view
- Create index
- Alter index
- Alter table
- Drop table
- Create table

## Data Query Language

When you are working in DQL, you are working with what many consider a really powerful aspect of what they are able to do with SQL, especially when you are working on a database system that is considered more modern. There is just one command that is needed in order to work with the DQL part, and this command is the "Select" command. You are able to use this command in various ways including using it to run queries when you are inside of a relational database. If you were interested in getting results that are more detailed, you would need to use the Select command through DQL to make this happen.

## Data Control Language

The DCL is another component of SQL that you should learn to use, and it is the commands that the user works with any time that they want to control who is allowed to get on the database. If you are dealing with personal information like credit card information, it is a good idea to have some limitations on who can get onto the system and get the information. This DCL command is used to help generate the objects that are related to who can access the information in the database, including who will be able to distribute the information.

There are a few commands that are helpful when you are working on DCL including:

- Create synonym
- Grand
- Alter password
- Revoke

## Data Administration Commands

When it comes to some of the commands that you can use inside SQL, you can also use them in order to audit or analyze the operation that is inside of the database. To access the performance of the database overall with the help of some of these commands. If you would like to fix something that is causing issues on the system or you would like to get rid of some of the bugs on the system, these are the commands that you are going to need to work with. While there are some options that you can choose from with these commands, the two most popular options include:

- Stop audit
- Start audit

One of the things that you need to remember when working with SQL is that data administration and database administration are going to be two different ideas inside the system. For example, database administration is going to be the part that will manage all your database, including the different commands that you are setting up in SQL and they will also be more specific to the implementation that is done in SQL.

## Transactional Control Commands

If you are trying to manage and keep track of some of the transactions that are going on with your database with you and the customer, the transactional control commands are the right ones to use. If you are a company that uses their website in order to sell products online, the transactional control commands are going to help make sure that you can keep all of this in line. There are several things that you will be able to use these transactional control commands for, including:

### *Commit*

This is the command that you will need to use in order to save information that relates to the different transactions that are inside your database.

### *Savepoint*

This is the command that you will be able to use in order to generate different points inside the group of transactions. This is also the one that you can use at the same time as the Rollback Command.

### *Rollback*

This command is the one that you will use whenever you are looking through the database, and you would like to undo at least one of the transactions inside.

## Set transaction

This command is the one that you can use any time that you are trying to take the transactions in your database and give them names. You will often use this one whenever you are trying to label things for a bit more organization.

All six of these types are going to be important based on the results that you would like to get out of your search. Each of these will be explored a bit more as we go through this guidebook so that you understand better how to use them, when to use them, and how to divide up the information in the proper way to avoid issues and to keep your database nice and organized with the help of the SQL language.

## c. how to install MySQL applications

MySQL is a tool (database server) that uses SQL syntax to manage databases. It is an RDBMS (Relational Database Management System) that you can use to facilitate the manipulation of your databases.

If you are managing a website using MySQL, ascertain that the host of your website supports MySQL too.

Here's how you can install MySQL in your Microsoft Windows. We will be using Windows because it is the most common application used in computers.

**How to install MySQL on Microsoft Windows in your**

Installing MySQL

- Download MySQL from the internet.
- Run the install file. You will be asked some questions, following which you should run the setup of the program.
- Troubleshoot MySQL.
- If the downloaded MySQL fails to work on your server, you will just have to buy a server running Mac OS X. Such servers will come with a pre-installed software and most of their configuration issues are already sorted out.

### d. how to launch MySQL Workbench

MySQL is a server program for querying databases, an open source relational database management system. It can be referred to as a client-server system. It is able to support a number of administrative tools, libraries, and programs, as well as, application programming interfaces.

This is a branded version of SQL. It allows its users to get data that they need from their databases, managing the database as well as receiving any reports pertaining to that database.

You can get it easily and for free from MySQL website, or you can choose to pay for a commercial release which comes with additional functionality.

MySQL runs on different platforms which include Windows, Mac OS X, and Linux. If it is possible, find and download it on your computer if you have a supporting platform. Some web hosting services provide it as their implementation as part of their package though, and each comes with a different interface to connect you to the database.

If you are using it as part of a website or application, those people that will visit the site will not have to download any additional software in order to use the features of MySQL.

**Its performance**

MySQL is written in C and C++, and it uses the kernel thread. This allows for multi-threading so as to take advantage of the many CPUs if they are available. It uses thread-based memory allocation which is joined by optimized nested-loop so as to improve its speed.

It uses hash tables as temporary tables whenever you are executing your queries. It uses SQL functions in an optimized class library in order to improve speed and reduce the need for accessing memory whenever you are querying tables in a database.

**MySQL databases**

With MySQL, you can add, access, modify and also delete any data that is stored within the database of a MySQL server.

The only limitation will be on the number of tables you can create, and all this depends on the file system.

If you have large MySQL databases, you can partition them so as to improve performance and management.

When you are querying, you are free to include tables from different databases on the same query.

**MySQL Tables**

There is a large amount of data that you can create with MySQL. You can create about 4,096 columns and store as many records as you want with no limitation at all whenever you are designing MySQL tables.

Each field can contain an assorted range of data. You can always fix the length of a certain field set primary and index keys, require that they have values and even increment numbers automatically.

SQL syntax is utilized to query tables. Use functions such as select, insert, update, show, join, and delete, among other syntaxes that are allowed by SQL languages.

**Connecting to MySQL server**

To add or modify any data that is located on MySQL server, you will have to connect to MySQL server. To succeed in this connection, you are required to have its hostname, port, username, and password.

**Creating MySQL database**

This is typically a simple and interesting thing to do once you master the basics of MySQL. Choose between phpMyAdmin interface or Secure Shell Command Line.

e. Writing the first MySQL code.

**When using phpMyAdmin:**

- Get onto the internet and log in to phpMyAdmin interface. Use the username and the password that is assigned to your web hosting provider.
- On the main frame of the page, click on 'Create New Database.'
- Choose and enter the name of the database that you want to create in the blank space that has been provided

- Click 'Create' and you will have created your database already. You will get a confirmation message stating your database is successfully created.

**When using SSH Command Line:**

- Go to the internet and log in using an appropriate SSH client. You will need a username and password that has been provided by your web hosting provider.

- Into the command line, enter mysql -uUSERNAME – pPASSWORD using your own username and password in capital letters.

- Choose a database name and enter into the prompt that will be provided.

- Create the database and wait for the confirmation that the database has been created.

# Chapter 2. DATABASE

## a. How to create a SQL database

Before you can be able to do anything on your data, create a database. My assumption is that you have installed either **MySQL** or **SQL Server** in your computer.

To create a database in SQL, we use the CREATE DATABASE statement. This statement takes the syntax given below:

CREATE DATABASE database_name;

First, login to MySQL by running the following command:

mysql -u root –p

Now you have logged into the MySQL database, it is time for you to create a new database. In the command given below, we are creating a database named *school* :

CREATE DATABASE school;

```
mysql> CREATE DATABASE school;
Query OK, 1 row affected (0.00 sec)
mysql>
```

The output shows that the database was created successfully. However, it will be good for you to confirm whether or not the database was created. To do this, use the **SHOW command** as shown below:

SHOW databases;

The above output shows that the school database was created successfully. The above command returns the list of databases you have in your system.

```
mysql> SHOW databases;
+--------------------+
| Database           |
+--------------------+
| information_schema |
| company1           |
| easydrive          |
| library_system     |
| movies             |
| mysql              |
| performance_schema |
| school             |
| sys                |
| wordpress          |
+--------------------+
10 rows in set (0.00 sec)

mysql>
```

An attempt to create a database that already exists generates an error. To confirm this, try to recreate the school database by running the following command:

**CREATE** DATABASE school;

```
mysql> CREATE DATABASE school;
ERROR 1007 (HY000): Can't create database 'school'; database exists
mysql>
```

The above output shows an error because the database already exists. To avoid this error, we can use the optional clause **IF NOT EXISTS**. This is showed below:

```
mysql> CREATE DATABASE IF NOT EXISTS school;
Query OK, 1 row affected, 1 warning (0.00 sec)
mysql>
```

The statement executed without returning an error.

Once you have created a database, it doesn't mean that you have selected it for use. You must select the target database using the

**USE statement**. To select the school database, for example, run the following command:

**USE** school;

After running the above command, the school database will receive all the commands you execute.

RENAME Database

Sometimes, you may need changing the name of a database. This is after you realize that the name you have given to the database is not much relevant to it. You may also need giving the database a database name. This can be done using the SQL **RENAME DATABASE command**.

The command takes the syntax given below:

**RENAME DATABASE** old_database_name **TO** new_database_name;

For example, in my case, I have the following list of databases:

```
mysql> SHOW DATABASES;
+--------------------+
| Database           |
+--------------------+
| information_schema |
| company1           |
| easydrive          |
| library_system     |
| movies             |
| mysql              |
| performance_schema |
| school             |
| sys                |
| wordpress          |
+--------------------+
10 rows in set (0.01 sec)

mysql>
```

Let us rename the database named *movies* by giving it the name *movies_db*. This means we run the following command:

RENAME DATABASE movies TO movies_db;

The database should be renamed successfully.

Database Backup

It is always important to back up your database. This is because an unexpected and unforeseen event may happen to the database. Examples of such unforeseen events include Cyber-criminality and natural disasters. In case of such an occurrence, it will be impossible for you to recover your database if you had not backed it up. However, if your database had been backed up, it will be easy to recover the database and resume normal operations. You also need to back up your database to prevent the loss of your data. SQL provides you with an easy way of creating a backup of your database.

To create a database backup, you use the **BACKUP DATABASE command**. This command takes the syntax given below:

BACKUP DATABASE database_name

TO DISK = 'file_path';

The *database_name* parameter denotes the name of the database you need to back up. The *file_path* parameter denotes the file leading to the directory where you need to back up your database. The above command should be done when you need to back up the database from the beginning.

However, you can use the *differential command* if you need to create a **differential backu**p. When you do this, the backup will only be created from the time you did your last full backup of the database. To do this, you must change the command to:

BACKUP DATABASE database_name

TO DISK = 'file_path'

WITH DIFFERENTIAL;

We have changed the command by adding the **WITH DIFFERENTIAL** statement. This means that the command will perform a differential backup on the database.

Suppose we need to create a full backup of the database named *school*. We will store the backup file in the local disk **D**.

The following command will help us accomplish this:

BACKUP DATABASE school

TO DISK = 'D:\schoolDB.bak';

If you need to create a differential backup of the database, just run the following command:

BACKUP DATABASE school

TO DISK = 'D:\schoolDB.bak'

WITH DIFFERENTIAL;

We have just added the **WITH DIFFERENTIAL** statement to the command.

Note that with a differential backup, the backup will be created within a short time. This is because you are only backing up changes that have occurred within a short period. However, a full backup will take a longer time to complete.

### b. how to use a database

This database is the one that you will want to use when you want to work with databases that are aggregated into logical units or other types of tables, and then these tables have the ability to be interconnected inside of your database in a way that will make sense depending on what you are looking for at the time. These databases can also be good to use if you want to take in some complex information, and then get the program to break it down into some smaller pieces so that you can manage it a little bit better.

The relational databases are good ones to work with because they allow you to grab on to all the information that you have stored for your business, and then manipulate it in a way that makes it easier to use. You can take that complex information and then break it up into a way that you and others are more likely to understand. While you might be confused by all the information and how to break it all up, the system would be able to go through this and sort it the way that you need in no time. You are also able to get some more security so that if you place personal information about the customer into that database, you can keep it away from others, in other words, it will be kept completely safe from people who would want to steal it.

## c. how to delete a database

So now, let's see how you can drop a database using the SQL Server's graphical user interface.

Right click on the name of any database that you want to delete (make sure you have created a test database for this exercise).

After you right click on the name of a database, you will see the delete option; click on it. A new window will open up; make sure you check the box that says close existing connections available at the bottom of the window. Closing existing connections allows you to safely delete your databases. With queries, this happens automatically, but when you delete your database using the GUI, you need to select this option so that if some project is using this database, the connection to that project will be closed before the drop option goes on. That's all you need to know about databases at this point of your learning curve. Let's move to the next chapter where I will talk about tables and operations related to tables.

## d. how to administrate the database

Let's see how to rename MySql and SQL Server databases.

Rename MySQL database

To rename the mysql database, you need to follow the following syntax:

RENAME DATABASE old_db_name TO new_db_name;


Rename SQL server database using T-SQL

This command is useful for SQL server 2005, 2008, 2008R2 and 2012.

**ALTER DATABASE** old_name **MODIFY NAME** = new_name

SQL SELECT Database

USE **DATABASE** database_name;

In oracle, you don't need to select database.

# Chapter 3. TABLES

Your tables are used to store the data or information in your database. They are composed of rows and columns as discussed in chapter 1. Specific names are assigned to the tables to identify them properly and to facilitate their manipulation. The rows of the tables contain the information for the columns.

## Create tables

**The following are the simple steps:**

**Step #1– Enter the keywords CREATE TABLE**

These keywords will express your intention and direct what action you have in mind.

> Example: CREATE TABLE

**Step #2–Enter the table name**

Right after your CREATE TABLE keywords, add the table name. The table name should be specific and unique to allow easy and quick access later on.

> Example: CREATE TABLE "table_name"

The name of your table must not be easy to guess by anyone. You can do this by including your initials and your birthdate. If your name is Henry Sheldon, and your birthdate is October 20, 1964, you can add that information to the name of your table.

Let's say you want your table to be about the traffic sources in your website, you can name the table"traffic_hs2064"

Take note that all SQL statements must end with a semicolon (;). All the data variables must be enclosed with quotation marks (" "), as well.

> Example: CREATE TABLE traffic_hs2064

## Step #3– Add an open parenthesis in the next line

The parenthesis will indicate the introduction of the columns you want to create.

> Example: CREATE TABLE "table_name"
> (

Let's apply this step to our specific example.

> Example: CREATE TABLE traffic_hs2064
> (

In some instances, the parentheses are not used.

## Step #4–Add the first column name

What do you want to name your first column? This should be related to the data or information you want to collect for your table. Always separate your column definitions with a comma.

Example: CREATE TABLE "table_name"

("column_name" "data type",

In our example, the focus of the table is on the traffic sources of your website. Hence, you can name the first column "country".

Example: CREATE TABLE traffic_hs2064

(country

## Step #4 – Add more columns based on your data

You can add more columns if you need more data about your table. It's up to you. So, if you want to add four more columns, this is how your SQL statement would appear.

Example: CREATE TABLE "table_name"

("column_name1" "data type",

"column_name2" "data type",

"column_name3" "data type",

"column_name4" "data type");

Let's say you have decided to add for column 2 the keyword used in searching for your website, for column 3, the number of minutes that the visitor had spent on your website, and for column 4, the particular post that the person visited. This is how your SQL statement would appear.

**Take note:**

- The name of the table or column must start with a letter, then it can be followed by a number, an underscore, or another letter. It's preferable that the number of the characters does not exceed 30.

- You can also use a VARCHAR (variable-length character) data type to help create the column.

- **Common data types are:**
    - **date** – date specified or value
    - **number (size)** – you should specify the maximum number of column digits inside the open and close parentheses
    - **char (size)** – you should specify the size of the fixed length inside the open and close parentheses.
    - **varchar (size)** – you should specify the maximum size inside the open and close parentheses. This is for variable lengths of the entries.
    - **Number (size, d)** – This is similar to number (size), except that 'd' represents the maximum number of digits (from the decimal point) to the right of the number.

    Hence if you want your column to show 10.21, your date type would be:

    number (2,2)

Example: CREATE TABLE traffic_hs2064
(country varchar (40),

keywords varchar (30),

time number (3),

post varchar (40) );

**Step #5 – Add CONSTRAINTS, if any**

CONSTRAINTS are rules that are applied for a particular column. You can add CONSTRAINTS, if you wish. The most common CONSTRAINTS are:

- o **"NOT NULL"** – this indicates that the columns should not contain blanks
- o **"UNIQUE"** – this indicates that all entries added must be unique and not similar to any item on that particular column.

In summary, creating a table using a SQL statement will start with the CREATE TABLE, then the "table name", then an open parenthesis, then the "column names", the "data type", (add a comma after every column), then add any "CONSTRAINTS".

## Deleting Tables

Deleting tables, rows or columns from your database is easy by using appropriate SQL statements. This is one of the commands that you must know to be able to optimize your introductory lessons to SQL.

**Here are steps in deleting tables:**

**Step #1– Select the DELETE command**

On your monitor, choose the DELETE command and press the key. Downloading Window's MySQL Database, MySQL Connectors and MySQL Workbench can facilitate your process.

Expert SQL users may laugh and say that these steps should not be included in this book. But for beginners, it is crucial to state specifically what steps should be done. Imagine yourself learning a totally new language; Russian for example, and you'll know what I mean.

**Step #2– Indicate from what table**

You can do this by adding the word "FROM" and the name of the table

    DELETE FROM 'table_name"

Make sure you have selected the proper table_name. Using our first sample example from the previous chapter, this is how your SQL statement would appear:

    Example: DELETE from traffic_hs2064

**Step #3–Indicate the specific column or row by adding "where"**

If you don't indicate the "where" all your files would be deleted, so ensure that your statement is complete.

Example: DELETE FROM 'table_name"

WHERE "column_name"

Hence, if you want to delete the entire table, simply choose:

DELETE FROM "table_name";

Using our previous example from chapter 1, this is how your SQL statement would appear:

Example: DELETE FROM traffic_hs2064

where time = (10)


DELETE from traffic_hs2064

where time = (5);


**Step #4–Complete your DELETE statement by adding the necessary variables**

Example: DELETE FROM "table_name"

WHERE "column_name"

OPERATOR "value"

[AND/OR "column"

OPERATOR "value"];

Deleting the wrong tables from your database can cause problems, so, ascertain that you have entered the correct SQL statements.

## Inserting Data into a Table

You can insert a new data into an existing table through the following steps.

**Step #1–Enter the key words INSERT INTO**

Select the key words INSERT INTO. The most common program, which is compatible with SQL is windows MySQL. You can use this to insert data into your table.

**Step #2 - Add the table name**

Next, you can now add the table name. Be sure it is the correct table

>Example: INSERT INTO"table_name"

>*Using our own table:*
>Example: INSERT INTO traffic_hs2064

**Step #3–Add Open parenthesis**

You can now add your open parenthesis after the table name and before the column_names. Remember to add commas after each column.

>Example: INSERT INTO"table_name"

>(

Using our own table:

>Example: INSERT INTO traffic_hs2064

>(

## Step #4–Indicate the column

Indicate the column where you intend to insert your data.

>Example: INSERT INTO"table_name"

>("column_name",. . . "column_name"

## Step #5– Close the columns with a close parenthesis

Don't forget to add your closing parenthesis. This will indicate that you have identified the columns accordingly.

>Example: INSERT INTO"table_name"

>("first_columnname", . . ."last_columnname")

## Step #6–Add the key word values

The key word values will help your selection be more specific. This is followed by the list of values. These values must be enclosed in parentheses too.

    Example: INSERT INTO"table_name"

        ("first_columnname", . . ."last_columnname")

        values (first_value, . . . last_value

**Step #7– Add the closing parenthesis**

Remember to add the close parenthesis to your SQL statement. This will indicate that the column does not go no further.

    Example: INSERT INTO"table_name"

        ("first_columnname", . . ."last_columnname")

        values (first_value, . . . last_value)

**Step #8–Add your semicolon**

All SQL statements end up with a semicolon, with the exception of a few.

    Example: INSERT INTO"table_name"

        ("first_columnname", . . ."last_columnname")

        values (first_value, . . . last_value);

Take note that strings must be enclosed in single quotation marks, while numbers are not.

Using our sample table, you can come up with this SQL statement:

Example: INSERT INTO "traffic_hs2064"

(country, keyword. time)

values ('America','marketing', 10);

You can insert more data safely without affecting the other tables. Just make sure you're using the correct SQL commands or statements.

## Dropping a Table

You can drop or delete a table with a few strokes on your keyboard. But before you decide to drop or delete a table, think about the extra time you may spend restoring it back, if you happen to need it later on. So, be careful with this command.

**Dropping a table**

Dropping a table is different from deleting the records/data in the table. When you drop a table, you are deleting the table definition plus the records/data in the table.

Example: DROP TABLE "table_name"

Using our table, the SQL statement would read like this.

Example: DROP TABLE traffic_hs2064;

**Deleting data in a table**

As discussed in the earlier chapters, this action will delete all the records/data in your table but will not delete the table itself. Hence, if your table structure is not deleted, you can insert data later on.

The complete steps in deleting data or record in a table are discussed in another chapter.

DROPPING your table is easy as long as you are able to create the proper SQL.

### Using the ALTER TABLE Query

There will be several times you need to use the ALTER TABLE command. This is when you need to edit, delete or modify tables and constraints.

The basic SQL statement for this query is:
Example:  ALTER TABLE "table_name"

    ADD "column_name" data type;

You can use this base table as your demo table:

Traffic_hs2064

| Country | Searchword | Time | Post |
|---------|------------|------|------|

| America | perfect | 5 | Matchmaker |
|---|---|---|---|
| Italy | partner | 2 | NatureTripping |
| Sweden | mate | 10 | Fiction |
| Spain | couple | 3 | News |
| Malaysia | team | 6 | Health |
| Philippines | island | 5 | Entertainment |
| Africa | lover | 4 | Opinion |

If your base table is the table above, and you want to add another column labeled City, you can create your SQL query this way:

Examples: ALTER TABLE Traffic_hs2064

    ADD City char(30);

The output table would appear this way:

    Traffic_hs2064

| Country | Searchword | Time | Post | City |
|---|---|---|---|---|

| America | perfect | 5 | Matchmaker | NULL |
| Italy | partner | 2 | NatureTripping | NULL |
| Sweden | mate | 10 | Fiction | NULL |
| Spain | couple | 3 | News | NULL |
| Malaysia | team | 6 | Health | NULL |
| Philippines | island | 5 | Entertainment | NULL |
| Africa | lover | 4 | Opinion | NULL |

You can also ALTER a table to ADD a constraint such as, NOT NULL.

Example:  ALTER TABLE Traffic_hs2064

   MODIFY City datatype NOT NULL;

This will modify all entries that are NOT NULL.

You can also ALTER TABLE to DROP COLUMNS such as, the example below:

Example: ALTER TABLE Traffic_hs2064 DROP COLUMN Time;

Using the second table with this SQL query, the resulting table will be this:

Traffic_hs2064

| Country | Searchword | **Post** | City |
|---|---|---|---|
| America | perfect | **Matchmaker** | NULL |
| Italy | partner | **NatureTripping** | NULL |
| Sweden | mate | **Fiction** | NULL |
| Spain | couple | **News** | NULL |
| Malaysia | team | **Health** | NULL |
| Philippines | island | **Entertainment** | NULL |
| Africa | lover | **Opinion** | NULL |

You can ALTER TABLE by adding a UNIQUE CONSTRAINT.
**You can construct your SQL query this way:**

Example: ALTER TABLE Traffic_hs2064

ADD CONSTRAINT uc_Country UNIQUE (Country, SearchWord);

In addition to these uses, the ALTER TABLE can also be used with the DROP CONSTRAINT **like the example below.**

Example: ALTER TABLE Traffic_hs2064

DROP CONSTRAINT uc_City;

Here are examples of CONSTRAINTS.

- **NOT NULL**

This constraint indicates that the NOT NULL values should not be present in the columns of a stored table.

- **CHECK**

This will ensure that all parameters have values that have met the criteria.

- **UNIQUE**

This ascertains that all values in the columns are distinct or unique.

- **PRIMARY KEY**

This indicates that the values in two or more columns are NOT NULL and simultaneously UNIQUE.

- **FOREIGN KEY**

This will ascertain that the values of columns from different tables match.

- **DEFAULT**

There is a specified DEFAULT value for columns. This may appear as blanks or appear as NULL.

Make sure you use these constraints properly to make the most out of your SQL queries.

# Chapter 4. DATA

The purpose of database systems is to store the data in tables. This data is supplied by application programs running on top of the database. SQL has the INSERT command that helps us enter data into a table for storage. The command creates a new row in the table.

The command the following syntax:

INSERT INTO tableName(column_1,column_2,...)

VALUES (value1, value2, ...);

Note that we have specified the name of the table to insert data into, followed by the names of columns in which we need to insert the data, then the data values that are to be inserted. If you need to insert data into all the columns of the table, there is no need for you to specify the column names. However, if you need to insert into some columns while skipping the others, specify the columns into which you need to insert data.

The following command shows how to insert data into all the columns of the table:

INSERT INTO EMPLOYEES VALUES (1, 'jOHN', 'John12', 26, 3000.00 );

```
mysql> INSERT INTO EMPLOYEES VALUES (1, 'jOHN', 'John12', 26, 3000.00 );
Query OK, 1 row affected (0.00 sec)
mysql>
```

The command ran successfully as shown above. This means that a row has been created in the table.

However, you may need to insert data into some columns only. This is the time you must specify the names of columns into which you need to insert the data.

Suppose we don't know the salary of the employee. We can insert data into the other columns as shown below:

INSERT INTO EMPLOYEES (ID, NAME, ADDRESS, AGE) VALUES (2, 'Mercy', 'Mercy32', 25);

```
mysql> INSERT INTO EMPLOYEES (ID, NAME, ADDRESS, AGE) VALUES (2, 'Mercy', 'Mercy
32', 25);
Query OK, 1 row affected (0.02 sec)

mysql>
```

The salary column has not been affected by the above command.

## Constraints in MySQL

Constraints are required to restrict the values that are stored in a particular field. You can limit the type of data entered into a table with the help of constraints. Constraints can be applied at column level and at table level. Constraints are defined when the table is created. The following are the constraints available to you with MySQL:

- **PRIMARY KEY: you have already used the Primary Key constraint while creating the family_data table. The primary key is required to accept unique data for one or more columns, for faster access of values stored in the database.**

- **NOT NULL: this constraint specifies that a particular cannot accept blank entry.**

- **UNIQUE: this constraint does not allow duplicate entry in a column.**

- **FOREIGN KEY: in relational database management systems, the link between two tables is created with the help of a FOREIGN KEY. The primary key of one table when used in another table for retrieving related records is called the FOREIGN KEY.**
- **CHECK: as the name suggests, this constraint is used to check whether a valid value has been entered as per the logical statement.**

- **DEFAULT: default is a value that must be fed into a column if no value is defined while inserting data.**

## Updating Data

Updating or changing data is one task you must learn and engage in as a beginner SQL learner.

The key word for this SQL query is UPDATE. You can follow the steps below.

### Step #1–Create your UPDATE syntax

Prepare your update SQL query or syntax by using the key word UPDATE.

    Example: UPDATE "table_name"

        SET "column_name1"= value1, "column_name2"= value2;

### Step #2–Add the WHERE clause

Be sure to include the WHERE clause to identify the columns to be updated, otherwise, all of your data will be updated.

    Example: UPDATE "table_name"

        SET "column_name1"= value1, "column_name2"= value2

        WHERE some _"column_name"= some_value;

### Step #3–Double check your SQL syntax

You must double check your statement before clicking the enter button. One error can cause problems in your database.

Let's practice making UPDATE SQL statements from the table below. The table below is on "Online Students".

Students

| StudentNo | LastName | FirstName | Age | Address | City |
|---|---|---|---|---|---|
| 1 | Potter | Michael | 17 | 130 Reed Ave. | Cheyenne |
| 2 | Walker | Jean | 18 | 110 Westlake | Cody |
| 3 | Anderson | Ted | 18 | 22 Staten Sq. | Laramie |

| 4 | Dixon | Allan | 18 | 12 Glenn Rd. | Casper |
| 5 | Cruise | Timothy | 19 | 20 Reed Ave. | Cheyenne |
| 6 | Depp | Adam | 17 | 276 Grand Ave. | Laramie |
| 7 | Lambert | David | 19 | 32 8th St. | Cody |
| 8 | Cowell | Janine | 18 | 140 Center St. | Casper |
| 9 | Kennedy | Daniel | 17 | 11 21st St. | Laramie |
| 10 | Budzinak | Leila | 20 | 24 Wing St. | Cheyenne |

## EXERCISE #1

Let's say you want to update or change the student "Walker, Jean" with a new address and city. How would you state your SQL query?

## ANSWER:

Your SQL statement should appear this way:

    Example:  UPDATE students

SET Address ='34 Staten Sq', City ='Laramie'

WHERE LastName ='Walker';

REMINDER: AGAIN, Always indicate the WHERE clause to prevent updating all the data in your table.

If you have submitted the correct SQL query, your resulting table will appear like this:

Students

| StudentNo | LastName | FirstName | Age | Address | City |
|---|---|---|---|---|---|
| 1 | Potter | Michael | 17 | 130 Reed Ave. | Cheyenne |
| 2 | Walker | Jean | 18 | 34 Staten Sq. | Laramie |
| 3 | Anderson | Ted | 18 | 22 Staten Sq. | Laramie |
| 4 | Dixon | Allan | 18 | 12 Glenn Rd. | Casper |
| 5 | Cruise | Timothy | 19 | 20 Reed Ave. | Cheyenne |
| 6 | Depp | Adam | 17 | 276 Grand Ave. | Laramie |
| 7 | Lambert | David | 19 | 32 8th St. | Cody |

| 8 | Cowell | Janine | 18 | 140 Center St. | Casper |
| 9 | Kennedy | Daniel | 17 | 11 21st St. | Laramie |
| 10 | Budzinak | Leila | 20 | 24 Wing St. | Cheyenne |

## EXERCISE #2

You want to update the address of Cowell, Janine to 20 18th St. Laramie City. What would your SQL syntax be?

Try creating your SQL statement without looking at the answer.

**ANSWER:**

UPDATE students

SET Address ='2018thSt.', City ='Laramie'

WHERE LastName ='Budzinak';

If your SQL query is correct, your table will be updated according to your recent input.

## Pivoting Data

Pivoting data is converting your data, which are presented in rows, into column presentations.

Through the use of PIVOT queries, you can manipulate the rows and columns to present variations of the table that will help you in analyzing your table. PIVOT can present a column into multiple columns. You have also the option to use UNPIVOT query. UNPIVOT does the opposite of what PIVOT does.

It is extremely useful in multidimensional reporting. You may need it in generating your numerous reports.

**How can you compose your PIVOT query?**

**Step #1–Ascertain that your SQL can allow PIVOT queries**

Is the version of your SQL server appropriate for PIVOT queries. If not, then you cannot accomplish these specific queries.

**Step #2 - Determine what you want displayed in your results**

Identify the column or data you want to appear in your results or output page.

**Step #3–Prepare your PIVOT query, using SQL**

Use your knowledge of SQL to compose or create your PIVOT query.

To understand more about PIVOT, let's use the table below as a base table.

ProductSales

| ProductName | Year | Earnings |
|---|---|---|
| RazorBlades1 | 2015 | 12000.00 |
| BarHandles1 | 2016 | 15000.00 |
| RazorBlades2 | 2015 | 10000.00 |
| BarHandles2 | 2016 | 11000.00 |

Let's say you want an output that will show the ProductName as the column headings. This would be your PIVOT query:

**Example #1:**

SELECT * FROM ProductSales

PIVOT (SUM(Earnings)

FOR ProductNames IN ([RazorBlades1], [BarHandles1], [RazorBlades2], [BarHandles2]) AS PVT

With the PIVOT query above, your ProductSales table will now appear like this:

#ProductNamesPIVOTResults

| ProductName | RazorBlades1 | BarHandles1 | RazorBlades2 | BarHandles2 |
|---|---|---|---|---|
| Year | 2015 | 2016 | 2015 | 2016 |
| Earnings | 12000.00 | 15000.00 | 10000.00 | 11000.00 |

You can also manipulate the table based on your preferences.

## Deleting data

This action will delete all the records/data in your table but will not delete the table itself. Hence, if your table structure is not removed, you can insert data later on.

The complete steps in deleting data or record in a table are discussed in another chapter.

DROPPING your table is easy as long as you can create the proper SQL.

# Chapter 5. SELECTING DATA

## Selecting rows and columns

Selecting a datum from your database can be done through the SELECT key. You only have to specify the data you want to select.

Step #1–Choose the SELECT statement

Choose SELECT to identify your SQL command.

Step #2– Choose the column

Choose the specific column where you want to retrieve the data.

    Example: SELECT"column_name"

Step #3–Use the asterisk * to select all columns

If you want to select all columns use *, or you can also choose as many columns as you want.

    Example: SELECT"column_name1"

        ["column_name2","column_name3"]

Step #4–Add FROM and the table name, where the data will come from

You can enclose the identified columns and where conditions with open and close square brackets [ ], but this is optional.

> Example: SELECT"column_name"
>
> ["column_name","column_name"]
>
> FROM 'table_name"
>
> WHERE "colum_name";

You can also write the above example in this way:

> Example: select column_name, column_name, column_name
>
> from table_name
>
> where column_name;

Step #5–Specify the"CONDITION"

You can specify the condition through the common operators that are presented in chapter 4.

Example #1: SELECT"column_name"

> ["column_name","column_name"]
>
> FROM 'table_name"
>
> [where"colum_name" "condition"];

You can also write the above example in this way: (no open and close square brackets)

Example #2: select column_name, column_name, column_name

from table_name

where column_name condition;

Example #3: SELECT"column_name"

[,"column_name", "column_name"]

FROM "table_name"

[WHERE "column_name"LIKE'Am'];

In the example above, all entries that start or match with'Am'will be displayed.

Example: SELECT"column_name"

FROM "table_name"

WHERE "column_name"='America';

In the example above, only the rows that exactly matches or equals'America'will be selected.

Reminder:

You can remove the double quotes when using the actual names of the tables and columns.

## Filtering rows and columns

Filtering data is an essential skill that you can learn as a beginner. There are various filtering activities that have been previously discussed in the past chapters by the use of the SQL keyword WHERE.

Filtering the data is similar to selecting the data you want to be displayed on your monitors.

WHERE indicates the content/file that can be found in your table.

Without the WHERE key word, your SQL query would be 'lost in space' not knowing what data to filter and select.

You can use the following steps to filter your data.

**Steps #1–Decide what data to filter**

Know specifically what date in your table you would like to filter. Once you have decided, go to the next step.

**Steps #2–Select the data**

Write your SQL query with the key word SELECT to indicate your selected data.

Make sure you have chosen properly. Inaccuracies in your query can produce wrong results.

You can write the SQL query like this:

Example:
SELECT"column_name1,'column_name2,"column_name3"

**Remember to separate the column names with commas.**

Using the table displayed below, compose your SQL query based on the stated premise.

Let's say you have chosen to filter all students below age 17, and want to display all students, who are older than 17.

How would you write your SQL statement?

Students

| Student No | LastName | FirstName | Age | Address | City |
|---|---|---|---|---|---|

| 1 | Potter | Michael | 17 | 130 Reed Ave. | Cheyenne |
| 2 | Walker | Jean | 18 | 110 Westlake | Cody |
| 3 | Anderson | Ted | 18 | 22 Staten Sq. | Laramie |
| 4 | Dixon | Allan | 18 | 12 Glenn Rd. | Casper |
| 5 | Cruise | Timothy | 19 | 20 Reed Ave. | Cheyenne |
| 6 | Depp | Adam | 17 | 276 Grand Ave. | Laramie |
| 7 | Lambert | David | 19 | 32 8th St. | Cody |
| 8 | Cowell | Janine | 18 | 140 Center St. | Casper |
| 9 | Kennedy | Daniel | 17 | 11 21st St. | Laramie |
| 10 | Budzinak | Leila | 20 | 24 Wing St. | Cheyenne |

You can write the SQL query like this:

Example: SELECT LastName, FirstName, Address, City

**Step #3–Indicate FROM what table the data came from**

After selecting the columns you want displayed, indicate FROM what table they should come from.

> Example: Example: SELECT LastName, FirstName, Address, City FROM Students

**Step #4–Add the WHERE clause**

This is significant in filtering data, so remember to always use the WHERE clause. What data do you want to filter?

In the above exercise, you want to display all students above the age of 17. Hence, your resulting SQL statement would appear like this.

> Example: SELECT LastName, FirstName, Address, City FROM students WHERE Age = > 17;

**Step #5–Always add the semicolon**

SQL queries or statement almost always end with a semicolon. The semicolon is already added to the example above.

## Updating Data

Updating or changing data is one task you must learn and engage in as a beginner SQL learner.

The key word for this SQL query is UPDATE. You can follow the steps below.

Step #1 – Create your UPDATE syntax
Prepare your update SQL query or syntax by using the keyword UPDATE.

Double check your SQL syntax
You must double check your statement before clicking the enter button. One error can cause problems in your database.

Let's practice making UPDATE SQL statements from the table below. The table below is on "Online Students".

Students

| StudentNo | LastName | FirstName | Age | Address | City |
|---|---|---|---|---|---|
| 1 | Potter | Michael | 17 | 130 Reed Ave. | Cheyenne |
| 2 | Walker | Jean | 18 | 110 Westlake | Cody |

| 3 | Anderson | Ted | 18 | 22 Staten Sq. | Laramie |
| 4 | Dixon | Allan | 18 | 12 Glenn Rd. | Casper |
| 5 | Cruise | Timothy | 19 | 20 Reed Ave. | Cheyenne |
| 6 | Depp | Adam | 17 | 276 Grand Ave. | Laramie |
| 7 | Lambert | David | 19 | 32 8th St. | Cody |
| 8 | Cowell | Janine | 18 | 140 Center St. | Casper |
| 9 | Kennedy | Daniel | 17 | 11 21st St. | Laramie |
| 10 | Budzinak | Leila | 20 | 24 Wing St. | Cheyenne |

EXERCISE #1

Let's say you want to update or change the student "Walker, Jean" with a new address and city. How would you state your SQL query?

**ANSWER:**

Your SQL statement should appear this way:

Example:  UPDATE students

SET Address = '34 Staten Sq', City = 'Laramie'

WHERE LastName = 'Walker';

REMINDER: AGAIN, Always indicate the WHERE clause to prevent updating all the data in your table.

If you have submitted the correct SQL query, your resulting table will appear like this:

Students

| Student No | LastName | FirstName | **Age** | Address | City |
|---|---|---|---|---|---|
| 1 | Potter | Michael | **17** | 130 Reed Ave. | Cheyenne |
| 2 | Walker | Jean | **18** | 34 Staten Sq. | Laramie |

| 3 | Anderson | Ted | 18 | 22 Staten Sq. | Laramie |
|---|---|---|---|---|---|
| 4 | Dixon | Allan | 18 | 12 Glenn Rd. | Casper |
| 5 | Cruise | Timothy | 19 | 20 Reed Ave. | Cheyenne |
| 6 | Depp | Adam | 17 | 276 Grand Ave. | Laramie |
| 7 | Lambert | David | 19 | 32 8th St. | Cody |
| 8 | Cowell | Janine | 18 | 140 Center St. | Casper |
| 9 | Kennedy | Daniel | 17 | 11 21st St. | Laramie |
| 10 | Budzinak | Leila | 20 | 24 Wing St. | Cheyenne |

EXERCISE #2

You want to update the address of Cowell, Janine to 20 18th St. Laramie City. What would your SQL syntax be?

Try creating your SQL statement without looking at the answer.

**ANSWER:**

UPDATE students

SET Address = '2018ᵗʰ St.', City = 'Laramie'

WHERE LastName = 'Budzinak';

If your SQL query is correct, your table will be updated according to your recent input.

## Creating Indexes

Creating indexes is also essential knowledge that you should learn as a SQL beginner.

These indexes are essential when searching for data or tables because they provide an immediate and efficient result to queries.

To save time and effort, create indexes only for tables that you often use.

**The basic CREATE INDEX SQL query is:**

Example: CREATE INDEX "Index_name"
ON "table_name"; (you can include the "colum_name", if you need that data)

Example: CREATE INDEX Studex
ON Students (Name, Age, City);

The SQL above will display all files - even duplicate files. If you want your result table to show only unique data, you can use the keywords CREATE UNIQUE INDEX, instead.

The basic SQL statement is similar with that of CREATE INDEX.

Here it is:

Example: CREATE UNIQUE INDEX "Index_name"

              ON "table_name"; (you can include the "colum_name", if you need that data)

Retrieve your tables quickly by using CREATE INDEX.

## Functions

User-defined functions often come to play when creating your Python codes. These functions can be used when you want a task or code done repeatedly. Functions can also help in maintaining your codes.

Keep in mind that you have also your built-in functions, which you can easily 'call', whenever you need them.

SQL has numerous functions that can be used to work with date and time values. Let us discuss them.

## MySQL Functions

**MySQL databases**

With MySQL, you can add, access, modify and also delete any data that is stored within the database of a MySQL server.

There is no limitation as to the number of databases that you can create on a MySQL server. The only limitation will be on the number of tables you can create, and all this depends on the file system.

If you have large MySQL databases, you can partition them so as to improve performance and management.

When you are querying, you are free to include tables from different databases on the same query.

**MySQL Tables**

There is a large amount of data that you can create with MySQL. You can create about 4,096 columns and store as many records as you want with no limitation at all whenever you are designing MySQL tables.

Each field can contain an assorted range of data. You can always fix the length of a certain field set primary and index keys, require that they have values and even increment numbers automatically.

SQL syntax is utilized to query tables. Use functions such as select, insert, update, show, join, and delete, among other syntaxes that are allowed by SQL languages.

**Connecting to MySQL server**

To add or modify any data that is located on MySQL server, you will have to connect to MySQL server. To succeed in this connection, you are required to have its hostname, port, username, and password.

**Creating MySQL database**

This is typically a simple and interesting thing to do once you master the basics of MySQL. Choose between phpMyAdmin interface or Secure Shell Command Line.

**When using phpMyAdmin:**

- Get onto the internet and log in to phpMyAdmin interface. Use the username and the password that is assigned to your web hosting provider.
- On the main frame of the page, click on 'Create New Database.'
- Choose and enter the name of the database that you want to create in the blank space that has been provided
- Click 'Create' and you will have created your database already. You will get a confirmation message stating your database is successfully created.

**When using SSH Command Line:**

- Go to the internet and log in using an appropriate SSH client. You will need a username and password that has been provided by your web hosting provider.

- Into the command line, enter mysql -uUSERNAME – pPASSWORD using your own username and password in capital letters.

- Choose a database name and enter into the prompt that will be provided.

- Create the database and wait for the confirmation that the database has been created.

## Joins

The databases used in industries have very complex structures. The data selection is often done from more than one table. Sometimes, tens of tables combine together to return a meaningful result set. To combine the records of multiple tables and select them, we use joins. Joins allow you to query data from multiple tables. There are six types of joins available in SQL:

- Inner Join
- Left join
- Right Join
- Full Join
- Self Join

Cartesian product

Before we move on towards discussing the details about all the types of joins, let's first create another SQL table inside the Employee database. The name of the table will be Customers. In our scenario, I am assuming that the database Employee contains the details of all employees in a retail store. This database also keeps the details about the customers who are served by its employees. Let's start with creating a customer table.

CREATE TABLE CUSTOMERS(

CustID INT    Identity(1,1)   NOT NULL,

CustNAME VARCHAR (20)    NOT NULL,

CustAGE INT        NOT NULL,

CustADDRESS CHAR (25) ,

CustSALARY DECIMAL (18, 2),

EmpFKID INT NOT NULL,

PRIMARY KEY (CustID),

FOREIGN KEY (EmpFKID) References Employee (EmpID)

);

***Output:***
Command(s) completed successfully.

The customer id in the customers table is an identity column. An identity column is a column whose value gets incremented automatically whenever a record is inserted into the table. This means that while writing an insert query for this table, you will not need to pass a customer id for each record. Another interesting thing about the customer table is the presence of a foreign key. A foreign key defines a relationship between two tables. In our case, we can use this foreign key to figure out which employee served which customer. Due to the presence of foreign key, the referential integrity constraint is in place.

## Union

The union keyword combines unique results of two select statements. Union keyword only works when the select statements involved bring result sets with the same structure (equal number of column and rows), the same order of column selection, and the same datatypes. The query below is combining the results of a left joined query and a right joined query using the UNION keyword.

Select EmpID as Employee_ID,EmpNAME as Employee_Name, EmpAGE as Employee_Age,

EmpADDRESS as Employee_Address, CustNAME as Customer_Name from

Employee LEFT JOIN CUSTOMERS On Employee.EmpID = CUSTOMERS.CustID

## ALIASES

Sometimes you need to rename a table to facilitate your SQL query. This renamed table are termed ALIASES.

They are only temporary and do not change the name of your base table in your databases.

ALIASES are useful when your SQL query uses more than one table; when you want to combine columns; when your column_names are long or vague and you want to change them for something simpler and clearer.

You can also use ALIASES when you want to define the functions in your SQL statement.

**Here is an example of a SQL query using ALIASES:**

**For tables:**

    Example: SELECT"column_name1,"column_name2"

        FROM"table_name"AS"alias_name"

        WHERE [condition];

**For columns:**

    Example: SELECT"column_name"AS"alias_name"

        FROM"table_name"

        WHERE [condition];

# Chapter 6. VIEWS

VIEWS are virtual tables or stored SQL queries in the databases that have predefined queries and unique names. They are actually the resulting tables from your SQL queries.

As a beginner, you may want to learn about how you can use VIEWS. Among their numerous uses is their flexibility can combine rows and columns from VIEWS.

**Here are important pointers and advantages in using VIEWS:**

1. You can summarize data from different tables, or a subset of columns from various tables.

2. You can control what users of your databases can see, and restrict what you don't want them to view.

3. You can organize your database for your users' easy manipulation, while simultaneously protecting your non-public files.

4. You can modify, or edit, or UPDATE your data. Sometimes there are limitations, though, such as, being able to access only one column when using VIEW.

5. You can create columns from various tables for your reports.

6. The VIEWS can display only the information that you want displayed. You can protect specific information from other users.

7. You can provide easy and efficient accessibility or access paths to your data to users.

8. You can allow users of your databases to derive various tables from your data without dealing with the complexity of your databases.

9. You can rename columns through views. If you are a website owner, VIEWS can also provide domain support.

10. The WHERE clause in the SQL VIEWS query may not contain subqueries.

11. For the INSERT keyword to function, you must include all NOT NULL columns from the original table.

12. Do not use the WITH ENCRIPTION (unless utterly necessary) clause for your VIEWS because you may not be able to retrieve the SQL.

13. Avoid creating VIEWS for each base table (original table). This can add more workload in managing your databases. As long as you create your base SQL query properly, there is no need to create VIEWS for each base table.

14. VIEWS that use the DISTINCT and ORDER BY clauses or keywords may not produce the expected results.

15. VIEWS can be updated under the condition that the SELECT clause may not contain the summary functions; and/or the set operators, and the set functions.

16. When UPDATING, there should be a synchronization of your base table with your VIEWS table. Therefore, you must analyze the VIEW table, so that the data presented are still correct, each time you UPDATE the base table.

17. Avoid creating VIEWS that are unnecessary because this will clutter your catalogue.

18. Specify "column_names" clearly.

19. The FROM clause of the SQL VIEWS query may not contain many tables, unless specified.

20. The SQL VIEWS query may not contain HAVING or GROUP BY.

21. The SELECT keyword can join your VIEW table with your base table.

# Chapter 7. What is a view, how to create a view, how to alter a view, deleting a view

**How to create VIEWS**

You can create VIEWS through the following easy steps:

Step #1 - Check if your system is appropriate to implement VIEW queries.

Step #2 - Make use of the CREATE VIEW SQL statement.

Step #3 – Use key words for your SQL syntax just like with any other SQL main queries.

Step #4 – Your basic CREATE VIEW statement or syntax will appear like this:

Example:  Create view view_"table_name AS

    SELECT"column_name1"

    FROM"table_name"

    WHERE [condition];

Let's have a specific example based on our original table.

EmployeesSalary

| Names | Age | Salary | City |
|---|---|---|---|
| Williams, Michael | 22 | 30000.00 | Casper |
| Colton, Jean | 24 | 37000.00 | San Diego |
| Anderson, Ted | 30 | 45000.00 | Laramie |
| Dixon, Allan | 27 | 43000.00 | Chicago |
| Clarkson, Tim | 25 | 35000.00 | New York |
| Alaina, Ann | 32 | 41000.00 | Ottawa |
| Rogers, David | 29 | 50000.00 | San Francisco |
| Lambert, Jancy | 38 | 47000.00 | Los Angeles |
| Kennedy, Tom | 27 | 34000.00 | Denver |
| Schultz, Diana | 40 | 46000.00 | New York |

Based on the table above, you may want to create a view of the customers' name and the City only. This is how you should write your statement.

Example: CREATE VIEW EmployeesSalary_VIEW AS

SELECT Names, City

FROM EmployeesSalary;

From the resulting VIEW table, you can now create a query such as the statement below.

SELECT * FROM EmployeesSalary_VIEW;

This SQL query will display a table that will appear this way:

EmployeesSalary

| Names | City |
|---|---|
| Williams, Michael | Casper |
| Colton, Jean | San Diego |
| Anderson, Ted | Laramie |
| Dixon, Allan | Chicago |
| Clarkson, Tim | New York |
| Alaina, Ann | Ottawa |
| Rogers, David | San Francisco |
| Lambert, Jancy | Los Angeles |
| Kennedy, Tom | Denver |
| Schultz, Diana | New York |

**Using the keyword WITH CHECK OPTION**

These keywords ascertain that there will be no return errors with the INSERT and UPDATE returns, and that all conditions are fulfilled properly.

Example: CREATE VIEW"table_Name"_VIEW AS

SELECT"column_name1","column_name 2"

FROM"table_name"

WHERE [condition]

WITH CHECK OPTION;

Applying this SQL statement to the same conditions (display name and city), we can come up now with our WITH CHECK OPTION statement.

Example: CREATE VIEW EmployeesSalary_VIEW AS

SELECT Names, City

FROM EmployeesSalary

WHERE City IS NOT NULL

WITH CHECK OPTION;

The SQL query above will ensure that there will be no NULL returns in your resulting table.

## DROPPING VIEWS

You can drop your VIEWS whenever you don't need them anymore. The SQL syntax is the same as the main SQL statements.

Example: DROP VIEW EmployeesSalary_VIEW;

## UPDATING VIEWS

You can easily UPDATE VIEWS by following the SQL query for main queries.

>Example: CREATE OR REPLACE VIEW"tablename"_VIEWS(could also be VIEWS_'tablename") AS
>
>SELECT"column_name"
>
>FROM"table_name"
>
>WHERE condition;

## DELETING VIEWS

The SQL syntax for DELETING VIEWS is much the same way as DELETING DATA using the main SQL query. The difference only is in the name of the table.

If you use the VIEW table example above, and want to delete the City column, you can come up with this SQL statement.

>Example: DELETE FROM EmployeesSalary_VIEW
>
>WHERE City ='New York';

The SQL statement above would have this output:

EmployeesSalary

| Names | Age | Salary | City |
|---|---|---|---|
| Williams, Michael | 22 | 30000.00 | Casper |

| Colton, Jean | 24 | 37000.00 | San Diego |
| Anderson, Ted | 30 | 45000.00 | Laramie |
| Dixon, Allan | 27 | 43000.00 | Chicago |
| Alaina, Ann | 32 | 41000.00 | Ottawa |
| Rogers, David | 29 | 50000.00 | San Francisco |
| Lambert, Jancy | 38 | 47000.00 | Los Angeles |
| Kennedy, Tom | 27 | 34000.00 | Denver |

**INSERTING ROWS**

Creating an SQL in INSERTING ROWS is similar to the UPDATING VIEWS syntax. Make sure you have included the NOT NULL columns.

Example: INSERT INTO"table_name"_VIEWS "column_name1"
WHERE value1;

VIEWS can be utterly useful, if you utilize them appropriately.

# Chapter 8. TRIGGERS

Sometimes there are cases when certain SQL operations or transactions need to occur after performing some specific actions. This is a scenario that describes an SQL statement triggering another one to take place. A trigger is simply an SQL procedure compiled in the database that executes certain transactions based on previously occurring transactions. Such triggers can be performed before or after executing a DML statement (INSERT, DELETE and UPDATE). Moreover, triggers can validate the integrity of data, maintain consistency of information, undo certain transactions, log operations, read and modify data values in different databases.

**Creating a Trigger** - Once a trigger has been created, it cannot be altered or modified anymore (you can just either re-create or replace it). How a trigger works depends on what conditions are specified – whether it will be executed all at once when a DML statement is performed or it will be run multiple times for each table row that is affected by the given DML statement. A threshold value or a Boolean condition can also be included, which will trigger a course of action when the specified condition is met.

The standard syntax for creating a trigger is:

CREATE TRIGGER **TRIGGER_NAME**

**TRIGGER_ACTION_TIMETRIGGER_EVENT**

ON **TABLE_NAME**

[REFERENCING **OLD_OR_NEW_VALUE_ALIAS_LIST**]

**TRIGGERED_ACTION**

**TRIGGER_NAME** - the trigger's unique identifying name

**TRIGGER_ACTION_TIMETRIGGER_EVENT** - the specified time or duration that the set of triggered actions will occur (either before or after the triggering event).

**TABLE_NAME** – the database table for which the DML statements have been specified

**TRIGGERED_ACTION** – indicates the actions to be performed once an event is triggered


Dropping a Trigger

The basic syntax for dropping or destroying a trigger is the same as dropping a table:

DROP TRIGGER **TRIGGER_NAME**;

# Chapter 9. VARIABLES AND STORED ROUTINES

## Variables

Python makes use of variables. As previously discussed, variables can contain a string of words, an integer (number) or other items. Hence, they act as containers.

**Step #1–Specify the value of your variable.**

In the example below, the value of your variable is 50.

**Example:**

Let's say you want your variable to be 50, you can enter this in your Python.

    **myVariable = 50**

This is for the Python version 3. The first letter is in the lower case and the first letter of the next words are in the upper case. This is termed the 'camel case declaration'.

You must remember that Python is case sensitive, so use the upper case and lower case letters whenever necessary.

    **myVariableTitle = 50**

**Step #2–Press 'enter'.**

After entering or assigning the value, you can press 'enter', and the value 50 will appear. This is your value.

You can make use of it in math operations to compute whatever you want to compute.

If your syntax is wrong, a syntax error appears in red ink, informing you of the mistake.

You can assign values to your variables by using the equal (=) sign. You have to name your variable before the equal sign and assign its values after the equal sign.

**Examples:**

    **name ="Billy"**

    **surname ="Trump"**

    **age = 45**

    **height = 5**

Your variables are: name, surname, age and height and the values assigned are: "Billy", "Trump", 45, and 5.

If you want to print your variables, you can create your statement or code this way:

    **name ="Billy"**

    **surname ="Trump"**

age = 45

height = 5

print name

print surname

print age

print height

See image below:

The original shell was used; thus, the variables are printed one by one by pressing your 'enter' tab/key.

Unlike if you open a 'New File', the results will be displayed all at once in a new shell:

```
>>>
>>> name="Billy"
>>> surname="Trump"
>>> age=45
>>> height=5
>>>
>>> print name
Billy
>>> print surname
Trump
>>> print age
45
>>> print height
5
```

If you decide to open a 'New File', the syntax/statement will appear this way:

```
name = "Billy"
surname = "Trump"
age = 45
height = 5

print name
print surname
print age
print height
```

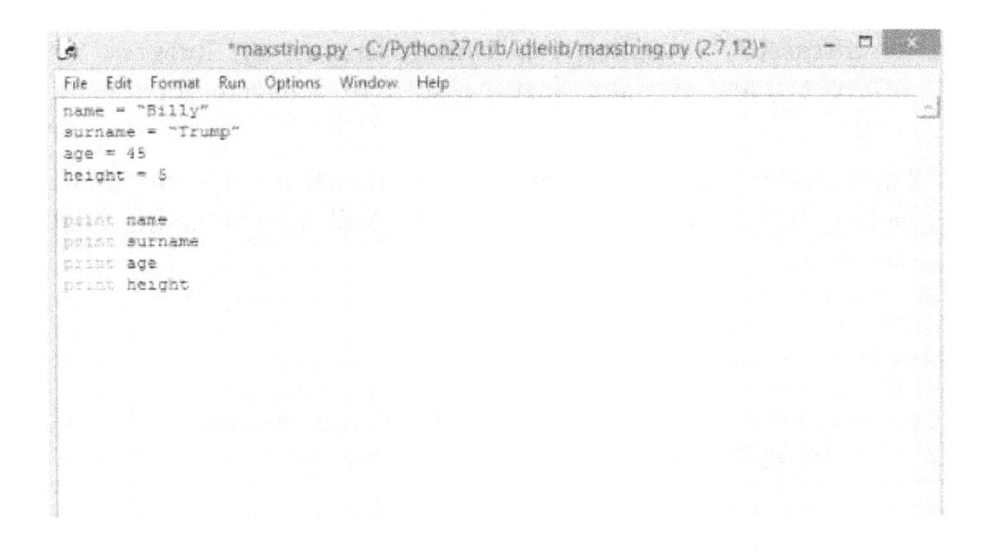

When you click 'Run', and then 'Run Module', the results will appear in a new shell:

```
Billy
Trump
45
5
>>>
>>>
```

**It's smart to name your variables according to their objects/content, so you won't get confused accessing them later on.**

As discussed, variables can contain names or integers, or different types of data. Just be sure to separate them with commas.

For variables that you want printed literally in a string, don't include them inside braces [ ]. These will appear in the final output.

Multiple assignments for variables

You can also assign, simultaneously, a single value to multiple variables. Here's an example:

Variables a, b, c, and d are all assigned to "1" memory location.

a=b=c=d=1

Another example is where variables are assigned individual values:

a, b, c, d, = 1, 2, "Potter", 3

The value of a=1

The value of b=2

The value of c = "Potter"

And the value of d = 1

Take note again, that numbers or integers are not enclosed in quotes (quotation marks– ''), while word-strings are enclosed in single, double quotes, or triple quotes. (' ', or" ", or""" """).

## Stored routines

Python contains built-in modules and functions that come with the program when you download it into your computer. Downloading the Python versions 2 and 3 in the same computer may not work, because some of their contents/functions are incompatible with each other, although they are both from Python.

The following are quick steps in accessing and learning these built-in modules and functions:

**Step #1– On your shell, type help('modules) and press'enter'.**

This command or function will provide all the modules of Python available in your downloaded Python.

When you press'enter', it will take a few seconds for the list of modules to appear.

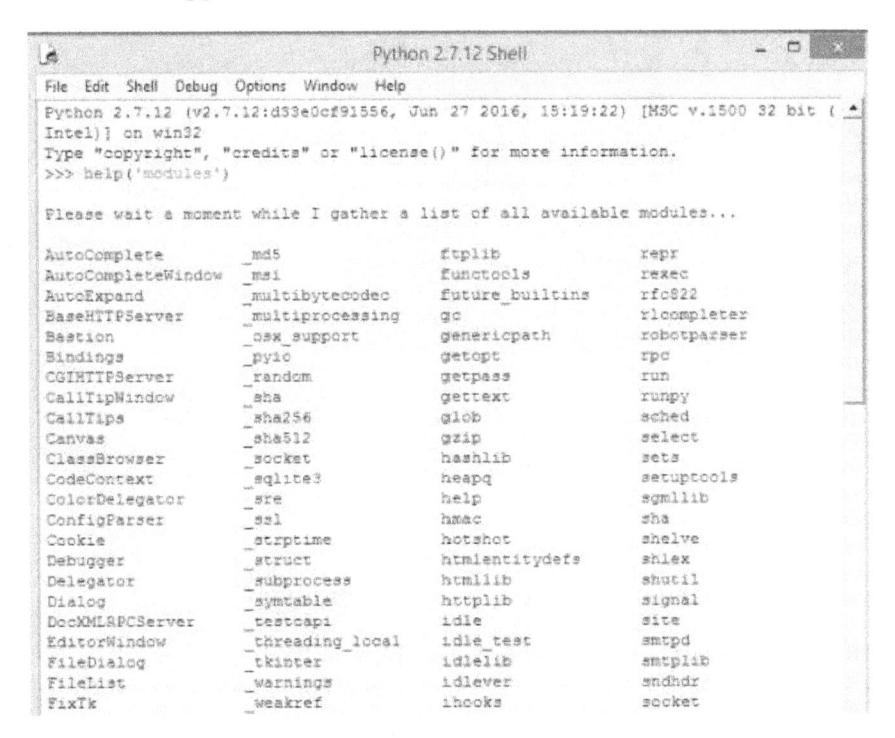

```
Python 2.7.12 Shell
File  Edit  Shell  Debug  Options  Window  Help
Python 2.7.12 (v2.7.12:d33e0cf91556, Jun 27 2016, 15:19:22) [MSC v.1500 32 bit (
Intel)] on win32
Type "copyright", "credits" or "license()" for more information.
>>> help('modules')

Please wait a moment while I gather a list of all available modules...

AutoComplete          md5                   ftplib                repr
AutoCompleteWindow    _msi                  functools             rexec
AutoExpand            _multibytecodec       future_builtins       rfc822
BaseHTTPServer        _multiprocessing      gc                    rlcompleter
Bastion               _osx_support          genericpath           robotparser
Bindings              _pyio                 getopt                rpc
CGIHTTPServer         _random               getpass               run
CallTipWindow         _sha                  gettext               runpy
CallTips              _sha256               glob                  sched
Canvas                _sha512               gzip                  select
ClassBrowser          _socket               hashlib               sets
CodeContext           _sqlite3              heapq                 setuptools
ColorDelegator        _sre                  help                  sgmllib
ConfigParser          _ssl                  hmac                  sha
Cookie                _strptime             hotshot               shelve
Debugger              _struct               htmlentitydefs        shlex
Delegator             _subprocess           htmllib               shutil
Dialog                _symtable             httplib               signal
DocXMLRPCServer       _testcapi             idle                  site
EditorWindow          _threading_local      idle_test             smtpd
FileDialog            _tkinter              idlelib               smtplib
FileList              _warnings             idlever               sndhdr
FixTk                 _weakref              ihooks                socket
```

**Step #3– Narrow down your search.**

You can narrow down the search by being more specific. You can specify the type of module you want to find. Let's say, you want to accessmodules about'profile', you can enter or type on your Python shell the following:

    **help("modulesprofile")**

And then press'enter'. The matching modules related to your designated search word will appear in your shell. See image below.

```
>>> help('modules profile')

Here is a list of matching modules.  Enter any module name to get more help.

_lsprof - Fast profiler
cProfile - Python interface for the 'lsprof' profiler.
hotshot - High-perfomance logging profiler, mostly written in C.
profile - Class for profiling Python code.
pstats - Class for printing reports on profiled python code.
test.profilee - Input for test_profile.py and test_cprofile.py.
test.test_cprofile - Test suite for the cProfile module.
test.test_profile - Test suite for the profile module.
test.test_sys_setprofile

>>>
```

The above image is only an example to demonstrate how to be more specific in your search for modules.

**Step #4 – Find the built-in functions and modules.**

You can access the Python built-in functions through your shell by typing the following:

dir(['__builtin__'])

See image below:

```
>>>
>>> dir(['__builtin__'])
['__add__', '__class__', '__contains__', '__delattr__', '__delitem__', '__delsli
ce__', '__doc__', '__eq__', '__format__', '__ge__', '__getattribute__', '__getit
em__', '__getslice__', '__gt__', '__hash__', '__iadd__', '__imul__', '__init__',
'__iter__', '__le__', '__len__', '__lt__', '__mul__', '__ne__', '__new__', '__r
educe__', '__reduce_ex__', '__repr__', '__reversed__', '__rmul__', '__setattr__'
, '__setitem__', '__setslice__', '__sizeof__', '__str__', '__subclasshook__', 'a
ppend', 'count', 'extend', 'index', 'insert', 'pop', 'remove', 'reverse', 'sort'
]
>>>
```

The different functions will appear on your Python shell. You can choose any of the functions you want to use.

You can also access the built-in functions or modules by importing them. This is done by opening your idle shell, and then typing:

import urllib

and then, type

dir(urllib)

101

When you press 'enter', all the Python modules will be displayed on your shell.

See image below:

**Step #5 – Find the uses of function words.**

You can now explore the uses/functions of the function words displayed on your shell. That is, if you don't know the function of the word.

Let's say you want to learn more about the uses of the function word 'max', you can use the help function by entering the following command:

>     help(max)

Press enter or execute. The use or functions of the word 'max' will be displayed on your shell, just like in the image below:

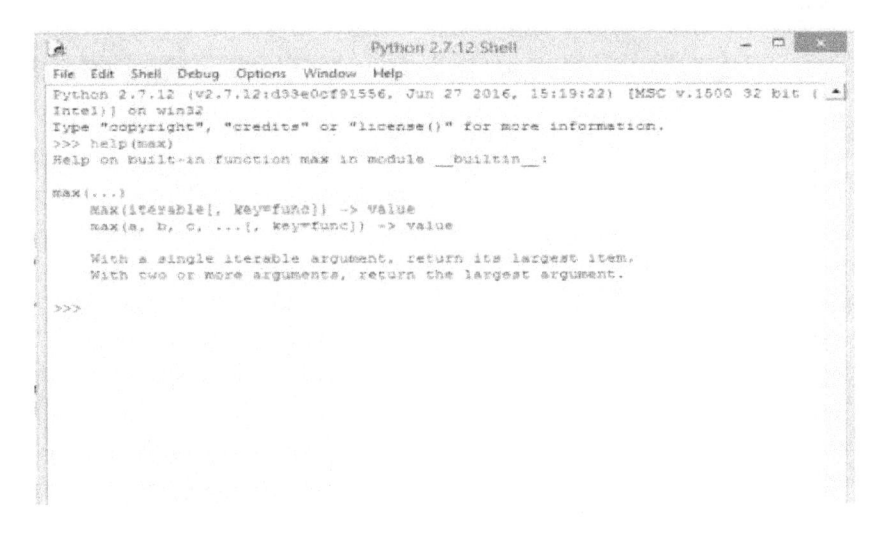

```
                         Python 2.7.12 Shell                    - □ x
File  Edit  Shell  Debug  Options  Window  Help
Python 2.7.12 (v2.7.12:d33e0cf91556, Jun 27 2016, 15:19:22) [MSC v.1500 32 bit (
Intel)] on win32
Type "copyright", "credits" or "license()" for more information.
>>> help(max)
Help on built-in function max in module __builtin__:

max(...)
    max(iterable[, key=func]) -> value
    max(a, b, c, ...[, key=func]) -> value

    With a single iterable argument, return its largest item.
    With two or more arguments, return the largest argument.

>>>
```

Based on the results in the image shown above, apparently, the function of 'max' is to show or display the largest item or largest (maximum) argument.

Therefore, if you want to know the largest item in a certain string, type max and then the values, and press enter.

The item with the highest value will be selected, just like the example below:

See image below:

```
Python 2.7.12 Shell
File  Edit  Shell  Debug  Options  Window  Help
Python 2.7.12 (v2.7.12:d33e0cf91556, Jun 27 2016, 15:19:22) [MSC v.1500 32 bit (
Intel)] on win32
Type "copyright", "credits" or "license()" for more information.
>>> help(max)
Help on built-in function max in module __builtin__:

max(...)
    max(iterable[, key=func]) -> value
    max(a, b, c, ...[, key=func]) -> value

    With a single iterable argument, return its largest item.
    With two or more arguments, return the largest argument.

>>> max(7,8,9,10)
10
>>> max(3,6,9,11)
11
>>> 
```

As shown above, the highest value of the first set is 10, and the second is 11.

### Step #5 - Access the Python modules and built-in functions from your downloaded file.

Another alternative is to access the different Python functions from the files that you have saved.

Remember, if your Python syntax or statement is wrong, the words will be colored red. So, it's easy to detect errors in your commands or statements.

## Stored procedures

You can create and save your Python files, so you can easily access and run them, whenever you need them. There are standard data types used in Python that you have to learn; these are: strings, lists, numbers, tuples and the dictionary.

But how do you create, save and run your own files?

Here's how:

**Step #1 – Open your Python shell.**

As instructed in the earlier chapter, after you have downloaded and saved the Python program in your computer/device, you can open your Python shell by clicking your saved Python and click IDLE (for Python version 3) or follow the instructions for version 2 as discussed in chapter 7.

**Step #2 – Click on the 'File' menu of your shell.**

At the left, uppermost portion of your Python shell, click the 'File' menu. The scroll down options will appear. Click on 'New File'. See image below:

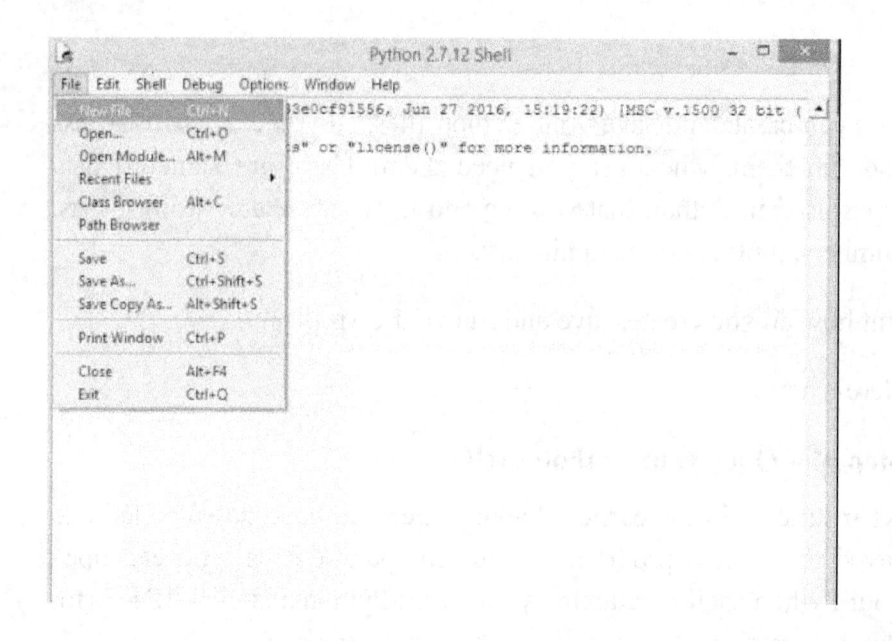

**Step #3 – Create your 'New File'.**

When you click on the 'New File' option, a blank box will appear. See image below:

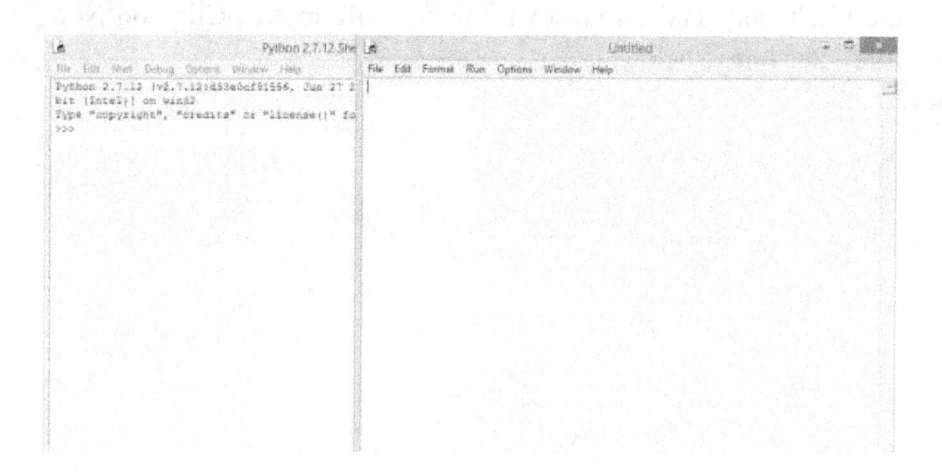

The new box is where you can create your file for saving. If you have noticed, the file is still untitled because you will be assigning the title before you can save it. You may save the file first before proceeding, or proceed to write your Python statement/code before saving.

Write your file.

For example, you want to create a file to provide the maximum or largest value of your variables (a, b, c, d), you can enter in your new file in the following manner:

**a=int(input("Please enter 1stnumber"))**

**b=int(input("Please enter 2ndnumber"))**

**c=int(input("Please enter 3rdnumber"))**

**d=int(input("Please enter 4thnumber"))**

**print (max(a,b,c,d))**

See image below:

```
a=int(input("Please enter 1st number"))
b=int(input("Please enter 2nd number"))
c=int(input("Please enter 3rd number"))
d=int(input("Please enter 4th number"))

print (max(a,b,c,d))
```

Make sure you enter the correct items and had used the necessary quotes and parentheses.

Any error in the signs, indentations, and quotes in your statement will yield errors.

Python won't be able to execute your command, and says so in red ink.

**Step #4 – Save your New File.**

You can save your 'New File' before writing it. Just access the 'File' menu, and choose 'Save As'.

See image below:

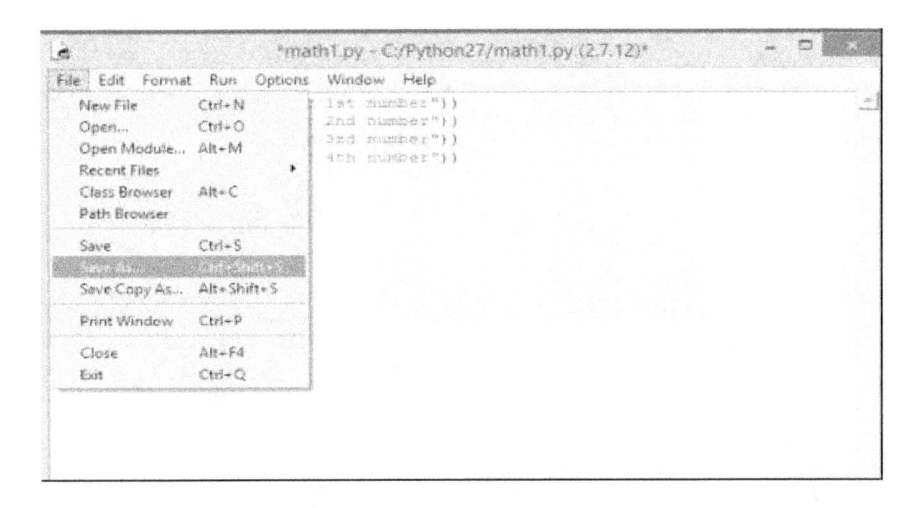

When you click on the 'Save As' option, a box will appear allowing you to select the name of your file, and where you want to save your file. Ascertain that your file is with the suffix .py.

Let's say you want to name your file math1. Type the name on the provided box, and press 'Save'.

See image below:

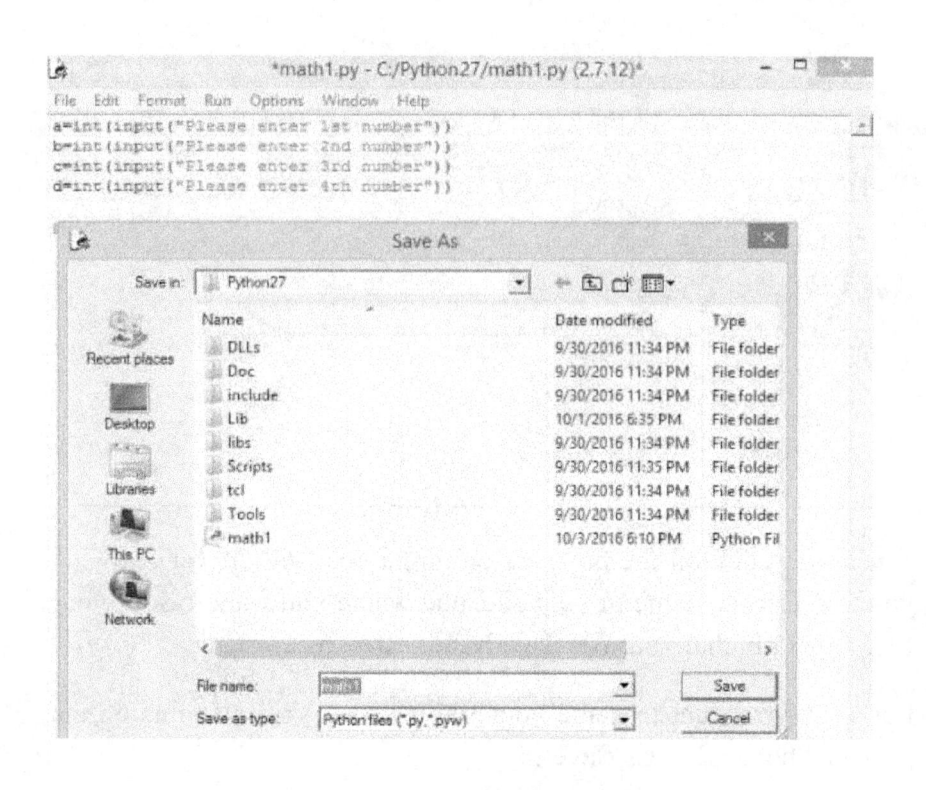

**Step #5 – Run your 'New File' (math 1) or module.**

You can now run your 'New File' by clicking on the 'Run' option, or key in F5 on your computer's keypads.

See image below:

```
math1.py - C:/Python27/math1.py (2.7.12)
File  Edit  Format  Run  Options  Window  Help
a=int(input("P     Python Shell         r"))
b=int(input("P                          r"))
c=int(input("P     Check Module  Alt+X  r"))
d=int(input("P     Run Module    F5     r"))
print (max(a,b,c,d))
```

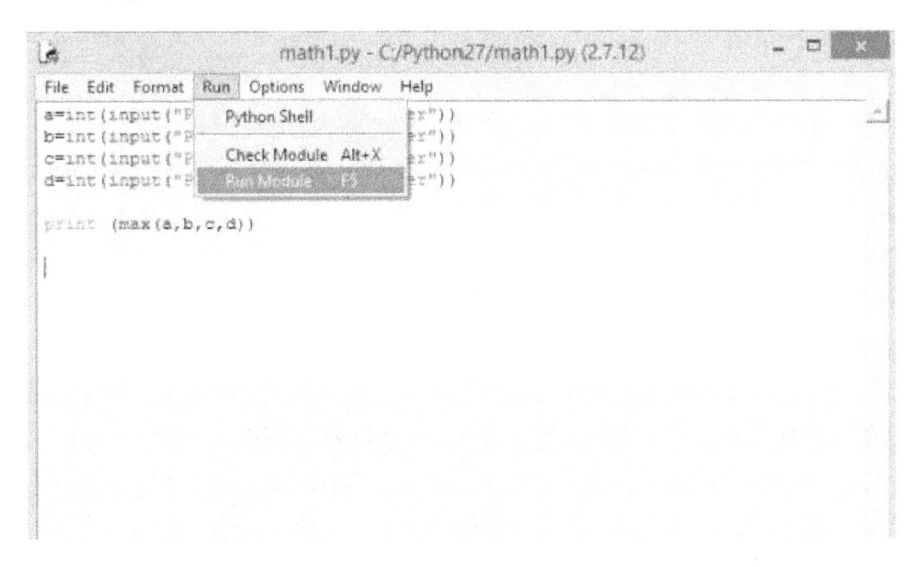

When you click on the 'Run Module' option, a new shell will appear. You can now enter your variables or values.

See image below:

```
 *Python 2.7.12 Shell*
File Edit Shell Debug Options Window Help
Python 2.7.12 (v2.7.12:d33e0cf91556, Jun 27 2016, 15:19:22) [MSC v.1500 32
bit (Intel)] on win32
Type "copyright", "credits" or "license()" for more information.
>>>
================================ RESTART: C:/Python27/math1.py ================================
Please enter 1st number
```

Test your file if it's working by providing the values required. Let's say the values of your items - a, b, c, and d -are 1356, 1827, 1359 and 1836. When you press 'enter', the value 1836 will appear, because it is the largest or highest value.

See image below.

```
Python 2.7.12 Shell
File Edit Shell Debug Options Window Help
Python 2.7.12 (v2.7.12:d33e0cf91556, Jun 27 2016, 15:19:22) [MSC v.1500 32 bit (
Intel)] on win32
Type "copyright", "credits" or "license()" for more information.
>>>
================================ RESTART: C:/Python27/math1.py ================================
Please enter 1st number1356
Please enter 2nd number1827
Please enter 3rd number1359
Please enter 4th number1836
1836
>>>
>>>
```

112

Of course, you can add more statements/codes, if you wish. This is just an example on how to create and save your Python file.

You can add another item/command, ("Please press enter to exit"), to provide easier access. Save your file again.

See image below.

```
a=int(input("Please enter 1st number"))
b=int(input("Please enter 2nd number"))
c=int(input("Please enter 3rd number"))
d=int(input("Please enter 4th number"))

print (max(a,b,c,d))

input("Please press enter to exit")
```

Remember to ALWAYS save any changes you made in your Python statement, and double check that your saved file is a .py file.

Take note that Python doesn't compile your programs, you have to run them directly.

**Deleting files**

113

To delete files, use the key 'del'.

>Example:
>
>**myname="Lincoln"**
>
>**myage=20**
>
>**del myname**

This will delete your variable 'myname', and whatever is specified in your command or code.

You can delete as many variables as you want. Don't worry, you can always create new files, if you want to.

## Stored functions

You can create and utilize your own user-defined functions.

**Step #1 – Use a keyword to define function.**

The function should be defined first making use of the word 'def', and then the name of its function.

When you want to define a function, you can use the general code below:

>def functionname (arg1, arg2, arg3)
>
>>statement1
>>
>>statement2
>>
>>statement3

Press 'enter' twice to access results.

Take note: arg stands for argument.

**Example:**

You are an employer, and you want to print the numbers (num) of your employees, thus, you defined 'employee' as the name of your file.

>def employee(num)

>print ("num")

See image below:

```
Python 2.7.12 Shell
File Edit Shell Debug Options Window Help
Python 2.7.12 (v2.7.12:d33e0cf91556, Jun 27 2016, 15:19:22) [MSC v.1500 32 bit (
Intel)] on win32
Type "copyright", "credits" or "license()" for more information.
>>>
>>> def employee(num) :
        print ('employee', num)
```

When you press enter, and input a number, the function will keep going until you decide to stop. So, the function can work repetitively. See image below:

```
Python 2.7.12 Shell
File Edit Shell Debug Options Window Help
Python 2.7.12 (v2.7.12:d33e0cf91556, Jun 27 2016, 15:19:22) [MSC v.1500 3:
Intel)] on win32
Type "copyright", "credits" or "license()" for more information.
>>>
>>> def employee(num) :
        print ('employee', num)

>>> employee (101)
('employee', 101)
>>>
>>> employee (301)
('employee', 301)
```

You can also create the Python syntax this way:

>    def employee(num)
>
>    print 'employee', num

Press 'enter' twice and then you can begin entering the numbers. The program will print it ad infinitum.

See image below:

```
Python 2.7.12 Shell
File Edit Shell Debug Options Window Help
Python 2.7.12 (v2.7.12:d33e0cf91556, Jun 27 2016, 15:19:22) [MSC v.1500 32 bit (
Intel)] on win32
Type "copyright", "credits" or "license()" for more information.
>>>
>>> def employee(num) :
        print 'employee', num

>>> employee (101)
employee 101
>>> employee (301)
employee 301
>>> employee (34)
employee 34
>>> employee (1)
employee 1
>>>
```

Functions can have no arguments, or have a couple of arguments. The arguments can be numbers, or strings.

You can also make use of the keyword 'return' to 'return' results (the 'return' key indicates that answers to the computation specified will be 'returned' – (displayed in the results).

**Example:**

If you want to obtain the average of the grades of students in 4 subjects, you can create the code this way: You can use this code for as long as you don't exit the shell. If you want to save it, you can create a New File so you could save it.

    def grades(a,b,c,d) :

        return ((a+b+c+d)/4)

See image below:

```
Python 2.7.12 (v2.7.12:d33e0cf91556, Jun 27 2016, 15:19:22) [MSC v.1500 32 bit (Intel)] on win32
Type "copyright", "credits" or "license()" for more information.
>>>
>>> def grades(a,b,c,d) :
        return ((a+b+c+d)/4)

>>>
```

When you, or the student enters his grades following the syntax/statement, the 'return' results would be the computed value already. See image below:

```
Python 2.7.12 Shell
File Edit Shell Debug Options Window Help
Python 2.7.12 (v2.7.12:d33e0cf91556, Jun 27 2016, 15:19:22) [MSC v.15
Intel)] on win32
Type "copyright", "credits" or "license()" for more information.
>>>
>>> def grades(a,b,c,d) :
        return ((a+b+c+d)/4)

>>>
>>> grades(80,79,81,84)
81
>>> grades(77,85,87,77)
81
>>> grades(90,88,86,85)
87
>>> grades(88,80,79,85)
83
>>>
```

The student has to type in the shell, after the arrows (>>>), following the given format:

**grades(80,90,85,75)**

Through this method, you can compute the grades of your students-ad infinitum.

Take note that 'return' results are different from 'return' statements. Refer to the chapter involved.

Keep in mind that you have first to define (def) the function, before your code can work, and print the results.

Remember to add the colon (:) after your def statement. You must also separate the arguments by commas.

In default parameters, the originally assigned value is printed, when the user doesn't enter any value.

In multiple parameters, an asterisk (*) can be used to indicate this.

Be adventurous and discover the joy of knowing how to make your codes work with Python.

## Deleting stored routines

Classes, as defined earlier, are data that contain objects that are related to each other. The functions that are applied to these classes are also related to each other.

The keyword 'self' is a sparring partner for class data because it's used in creating your class statements.

For classes to be used correctly, it's important to create correct Python statements and syntax.

How do use your classes? Here's how.

For example, you're the 'big boss' of a company, and you want to compile the personal information of your employees, you can create a Python class code to do this.

**Step #1 – Use the 'class' keyword.**

Open a New File and save it. Use the 'class' keyword in introducing your class code.

**Step #2 – Add the name of your 'class'.**

Add the name of your class (file name). Since the data is the personal information of your employees, you may want to name it - PersonnelInfo .

**Step #3 – Add the colon at the end of the first statement.**

Hence, it will appear this way: class PersonnelInfo :

**Step #4 – Define your variables**

You have to define or assign variables to your data. You need to use the word 'self' to indicate that the code is referring to the class.

In general, a class statement appears this way:

> class ClassName :
>
> > <statement-1>
> >
> > .
> >
> > .
> >
> > .
> >
> > <statement – last>

## Step #5 – Run your module.

See image below:

e

```
classcode.py - C:/Python27/Lib/idlelib/classcode.py (2.7.12)
File  Edit  Format  Run  Options  Window  Help
class Employee    Python Shell
    def person                        e, lastName) :
        self.f    Check Module Alt+X
        self.l    Run Module      F5
    def printPersonalInfo(self) :
        print(self.firstName, " ", self.lastName, " ")

employeeName=EmployeeInfo ()
employeeName.personalInfo("Virginia", "Walker")
employeeName.printPersonalInfo()
```

## Two types of class object operations

1. **Class instantiation** – this type utilizes function notations in calling a class object. A special method, (double underscore)__init__(double underscore) ( ) (bracket), can be defined by a class. __init__ is called a class constructor and it's used to initialize (init) a

120

value. Python uses this keyword to indicate (initialization).

**Example:**

def __init__ self :

self.data = [ ]

The class instantiation using the __init__ ( ) method, automatically raises __init__( ) for the newly formed class instance.

```
class EmployeeInfo:
    def __init__ (self) :
        print ("Employee Information Data.")
    def personalInfo(self, firstName, lastName) :
        self.firstName=firstName
        self.lastName=lastName
    def printPersonalInfo(self) :
        print(self.firstName, ' ', self.lastName, ' ')

employeeName=EmployeeInfo ()
employeeName.personalInfo('Virginia', 'Walker')
employeeName.printPersonalInfo()
```

Save and click 'Run', and then 'Run Module'.

When you click 'Run Module', a new shell will be opened with this image:

You can now enter your employees' names. See image below.

```
Python 2.7.12 Shell
File Edit Shell Debug Options Window Help
Python 2.7.12 (v2.7.12:d33e0cf91556, Jun 27 2016, 15:19:22) [MSC v.1500 32 bit (
Intel)] on win32
Type "copyright", "credits" or "license()" for more information.
>>>
============ RESTART: C:/Python27/Lib/idlelib/classcode.py ==============
Employee Information Data.
('Virginia', ' ', 'Walker', ' ')
>>> 'Donnie, Tell'
'Donnie, Tell'
>>> 'Venus', 'Potter'
('Venus', 'Potter')
>>> ('Miriam', 'Wells')
('Miriam', 'Wells')
>>>
```

We have also what we call 'destructors' represented by the Python keyword __del__( ): (double underscore + del + double underscore + brackets + colon.

This function will destroy or delete specified data or acts as a trash can for the data. Just like __init__, it automatically functions even without 'calling' it out.

```
*classcode.py - C:/Python27/Lib/idlelib/classcode.py (2.7.12)*
File Edit Format Run Options Window Help
class EmployeeInfo:
    def __init__ (self) :
        print ("Employee Information Data.")
    def __del__ (self) :
        print ("Employee Information Data is discontinued")
    def personalInfo(self, firstName, lastName) :
        self.firstName=firstName
        self.lastName=lastName
    def printPersonalInfo(self) :
        print(self.firstName, ' ', self.lastName, ' ')

employeeName=EmployeeInfo ()
employeeName.personalInfo('Virginia', 'Walker')
employeeName.printPersonalInfo()
```

If you use the del keyword in the object or instance, for example:

Adding employeeName.__del__ ( )

The resources or employees' name will be deleted or destroyed.

See image below:

```
*classcode.py - C:/Python27/Lib/idlelib/classcode.py (2.7.12)*
File  Edit  Format  Run  Options  Window  Help
class employeeInfo:
    def __init__ (self) :
        print ("Employee Information Data.")
    def __del__ (self) :
        print ("Employee Information Data is discontinued")
    def personalInfo(self, firstName, lastName) :
        self.firstName=firstName
        self.lastName=lastName
    def printPersonalInfo(self) :
        print(self.firstName, ' ', self.lastName, ' ')

employeeName=EmployeeInfo ()
employeeName.personalInfo('Virginia', 'Walker')
employeeName.printPersonalInfo()
employeeName.__del__()
```

When you click 'Run', and then 'Run Module', a new shell will open.

See image below:

```
Python 2.7.12 Shell
File  Edit  Shell  Debug  Options  Window  Help
Python 2.7.12 (v2.7.12:d33e0cf91556, Jun 27 2016, 15:19:22) [MSC v.1500 32 bit (Intel)] on win32
Type "copyright", "credits" or "license()" for more information.
>>>
============== RESTART: C:/Python27/Lib/idlelib/classcode.py ==============
Employee Information Data.
('Virginia', ' ', 'Walker', ' ')
Employee Information Data is discontinued
>>>
```

When you click 'Run', and then 'Run Module', another Python shell will open, printing the results. See image below:

```
Python 2.7.12 (v2.7.12:d33e0cf91556, Jun 27 2016, 15:19:22) [MSC v.1500 32 bit (
Intel)] on win32
Type "copyright", "credits" or "license()" for more information.
>>>
================== RESTART: C:/Python27/init1.py ==================
Virginia Walker
Apt. G, Reed Avenue, Cheyenne, Wyoming
>>>
```

You can edit your code to produce results that are in congruence with your preferences. Isn't it fun?

**Reminders:**

For each definition, a colon ( : ) is added at the end of the statement.

'self' is always included in each member function, even if there are no arguments. Example of arguments are those values found inside the parentheses (self, firstName, LastName).

Double quotes or single quotes can be used with the arguments.

The constructor and destructor can contain arguments other than self. You can include any arguments you want. Example of arguments are (self, firstName, lastName). Make sure though that your __init__ arguments are included in the instances or objects' statements that come after the 'def'.

2. **Attribute references** – this type uses the 'object.name' of common Python syntax. Whenever you define a

function of a class always pass an argument on 'self'. This is because the 'self' is pointing to the class.

**Example:**

We will be using the same code above – without the __init__ function. If you want the data about your employees, you can create your code this way:

```
class EmployeeInfo:
    def personalInfo(self, firstName, lastName) :
        self.firstName=firstName
        self.lastName=lastName
    def printPersonalInfo(self) :
        print(self.firstName, " ", self.lastName, " ")

employeeName=EmployeeInfo ()
employeeName.personalInfo("Virginia", "Walker")
employeeName.printPersonalInfo()
```

In the example above, in each definition (def) of a class, 'self' is always added for every function of the class. Notice also the indentations for the 'def' statements.

The following entries are not indented because the statements are not part of the definition of the class, but they are objects, or instances of the class.

employeeName=EmployeeInfo ( )

employeeName.personalInfo("Virginia", "Walker")

employeeName.printPersonalInfo ( )

If you run the class code above, this would appear in your Python shell:

```
Python 2.7.12 Shell
File Edit Shell Debug Options Window Help
Python 2.7.12 (v2.7.12:d33e0cf91556, Jun 27 2016, 15:19:22) [MSC v.1500 32 bit (
Intel)] on win32
Type "copyright", "credits" or "license()" for more information.
>>>
=============== RESTART: C:/Python27/Lib/idlelib/classcode.py ===============
('Virginia', ' ', 'Walker', ' ')
>>>
```

Tweak the codes and see what happens. Curiosity doesn't always kill the cat.

# Chapter 10. CONTROL FLOW TOOLS

## IF statement

In Python, you can use various condition statements. However, you have to ascertain that you follow the Python syntax rules and indentation. One of these rules is to provide an indentation after the 'if' and 'else' statements, when you enter their codes. Simply press the tab once to provide the indentation.

Anyway, the program will assist you in determining errors in your Python syntax. If there's an error, it will display the errors, and what's wrong with them. You can also press for help, if you're lost in the sea of Python lingo.

Therefore, relax and enjoy the experience.

Functions

The 'IF ELSE' statements, which execute codes, are generally used to compare values, or determine their correctness. 'if' is expressed, if the condition is 'true', while 'else' is expressed when the condition is 'false'.

General code is:

    if expression:

        Statement/s

  else:

        Statement/s

Example:

Assign a base statement first. Let's say you're teaching chemistry to freshmen college students and you want to encourage them to attend your tutorials. You can compose this Python code:

```
hours = float(input('How many hours can you allot for your chemistry tutorials?'))
if hours < 1:
    print ('You need more time to study.')
else:
    print ('Great! Keep it up!')
print ('Chemistry needs more of your time.')
```

## CASE statement

Ruby language is common in organizations for web application development. Ruby on Rails is a framework that allows for rapid development, and business teams focus on other business processes instead of coding functions from scratch. This framework provides a separator known as MVC structure (Model-view-controller). The MVC provides support in separating data, user interface, and business functions.

On the other hand, Python has the most popular MVC frameworks known as Django web framework for web application development. In addition, Python is also famous beyond the domains of web applications. For example, the Pandas library is useful for data preparation. Other libraries such as numpy and stats-model are also supportive in this case. Matplotlib is a powerful Python library for data visualization. Tensorflow is popular for machine learning tasks and projects. Besides, SciPy is another open-source library for Python, which is used for scientific computing and solving math functions that used to make engineering students sweat.

## WHILE statement

The **while** statement is the main looping statement and is mostly used whenever simple iterations are required. Its structure is as follows:

Counter = 10

while counter>0:

   print counter

   counter = counter-1

print 'Backward counting from 10 to 1'

This simple **while** loop will keep on checking the **while** condition again and again until the condition becomes false. Until the condition becomes false, every time the cycle goes through the loop. Then after the condition becomes false the interpreter resumes the former activity and continues with the program statements just after the loop. Following diagram illustrates the flow of while controls.

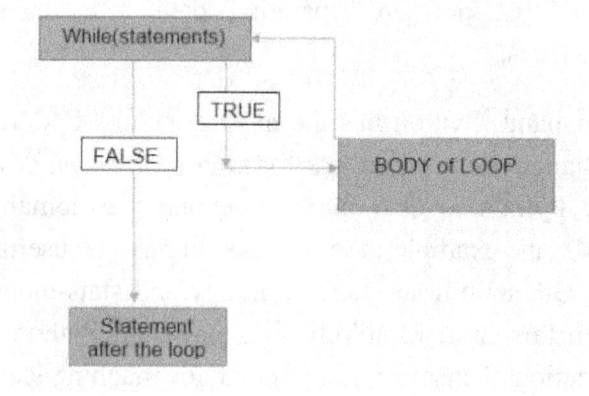

## LOOP statement

As defined in the previous chapter, it is a symbol used to represent repeated (iterated) word/s or sentence/s in Python programming. Anything that is being repeatedly used can employ a loop (a piece of code). Hence, it facilitates the task that you would want to accomplish.

**Types of loops**

1. **The 'while' loop** – this is used to implement a piece of code repeatedly.

**Example:**

Let's say you have these values: a – for individual numbers; t – for sum of the numbers:

a=1

t=0

And you want the user to 'Enter numbers to add to the total.', you write the code for the 'while; loop this way:

**print ('Enter numbers to add to the total.')**

**print ('Enter x to quit.')**

**(Now use the 'while' function to allow the action to become repetitive.)**

while a ! = 0:

print ('Current Total: ' , t)

a = float(input("Number? '))

a = float (a)

t+ = a

print ('Grand Total = ' , t)

This is how your code will look like.

# Chapter 11. CURSORS

In general, SQL commands manipulate, or work around, database objects using set-based operations, meaning transactions are performed on a block or group of data. A cursor, on the other hand, retrieves and processes a subset of data from the database one row at a time. It is actually like a pointer that refers to a specific table row. When cursor is activated, a user can select, update or delete the row at which it is pointing. It also enables the SQL program to retrieve table rows one at a time and send it to a procedural code for processing. In this way, the entire table is processed row by row.

To use the cursor functionality, its existence is declared first using a compound statement that could also be destroyed upon exit. The following is the standard syntax for declaring a cursor (but may differ for every SQL implementation):

Syntax:

DECLARE CURSOR **CURSOR_NAME**

IS {**SELECT_STATEMENT**}

After the cursor has been declared or defined, the following operations can now be performed:

**Opening a Cursor** - Once declared, the OPEN operation can be executed to gain access to the cursor, followed by the specified SELECT statement. The results of the database query will be saved in a certain area in the memory. The following is the standard format of the syntax when opening a cursor:

OPEN **CURSOR_NAME**;

**Fetching Data from a Cursor** - The FETCH statement is executed if the query results are to be retrieved after opening the cursor. The following is the standard syntax for fetching data from a cursor:

FETCH NEXT FROM **CURSOR_NAME** [INTO **FETCH_LIST**]

The statement inside the square brackets is optional, which will let you allocate the data fetched into a particular variable.

**Closing a Cursor** - There is a corresponding CLOSE statement that can be executed when you have opened a particular cursor. All the names and resources used will be released once the cursor has been closed. Thus, it is no longer available or usable in the program. The following is the standard syntax when a cursor is to be closed:

CLOSE **CURSOR_NAME**

# Chapter 12. Common beginner mistakes and how to fix them

Achieving an error-free implementation or design is considered to be one of the ultimate goals in handling any programming language. A database user can commit errors by simply performing inappropriate naming conventions, writing improperly the programming syntax (typographical errors like a missing apostrophe/parenthesis) or even when the data value entered does not correspond to the data type being defined.

To simplify things, SQL has SQL has created a way to return error messages so that users or programmers will be aware of what is happening in the database system. This will further lead to taking corrective measures to improve the situation. Some of the common error-handling error-handling features are the WHENEVER clause and the SQLSTATE status parameter.

**SQLSTATE**

The host variable or status parameter SQLSTATE is one of the SQL error-handling tools that includes a wide selection of anomalous programming conditions. It is a five-character string that consists of uppercase letters from A to Z and numeral values from 0 to 9. The first two characters refer to the class code, while the next three signify the subclass code. The indicated class code is responsible for identifying the status after an SQL statement has been completed – whether it is successful or not. If the execution of the SQL statement is not successful, then one of the major types of error conditions will be returned. Additional information about the execution of the SQL statement is also indicated in the subclass code.

The SQLSTATE is always updated after every operation. If its value is set to **'00000'**, this means that the execution was successful, and you can proceed to the succeeding operation. If it contains a string other than the five zeroes, then the user has to check his programming codes to correct the error committed. There are multiple ways on how to handle a certain SQL error, which normally depends on the on the class and subclass codes indicated by the SQLSTATE.

WHENEVER Clause

Another error-handling mechanism tool, the WHENEVER clause focuses on execution exceptions. Through this, an error is acknowledged and provides the programmer an option to rectify it. This is a lot better instead of not doing anything if an error occurs. If you cannot correct or reverse the error that was committed, then the application program can just be gracefully terminated.

The WHENEVER clause should be written before the executable part of the SQL code, in the declaration section to be exact. The standard syntax for the said clause is:

**WHENEVER** CONDITION ACTION;

**CONDITION** – the value can either be set to **'SQLERROR'** (will return TRUE if the class code value is not equivalent to **00, 01** or **02**) or **'NOT FOUND'** (will return TRUE if the SQLSTATE value is equivalent to 02000)

**ACTION** – the value can either be set to **'CONTINUE'** (program execution is continued as per normal) or **'GOTO address'** (a designated program address is executed)

# Chapter 13. Tips and tricks of SQL

SQL stands for structured query language. This language is a domain specific language that you are going to use if you are programming or trying to manage data inside of a RDBMS (relational database management system).

SQL was started with math, both tuple relational calculus and relational algebra. There is a lot of data definitions and manipulations along with control language that is going to be inside of SQL. SQL involves the use of things such as delete, update, insert, and query.

In essence, you are going to be able to update, delete, insert, and search for the things that you are going to be putting into the program. It is very common for SQL to be described as a declarative language, however, the program also allows for procedural elements.

This is one of the first languages that was able to use the relational model that was created by Edgar F Codd. Although it is not going to work with all of the rules that are set forth for this model, it is one of the most widely used languages for data bases.

In '86, SQL became part of the ANSI. Then, in '87 it became part of the ISO. However, there have been updates since then that have made it to where the language can include larger sets. Just keep in mind that the code for SQL is not going to be one hundred percent portable between data bases unless there are some adjustments to the code so that it fits the requirements for that data base.

Learning SQL can be one of the better decisions that you make about your career because you can push yourself forward with it that way that you can rely on using your own knowledge rather than having to go to someone else for their knowledge. In fact, people are going to be coming to you to learn what it is that you know about the program.

By learning SQL, you are going to be able to do more than you may have been able to before. Here are a few things that are going to give you a good reason as to why you should learn SQL.

Money

Learning SQL makes it to where you have the opportunity to earn some extra money. Developers that work with SQL earn around $92,000 a year! An administrator for an SQL data base is going to make about $97,000 a year. So, just learning SQL makes it to where you are able to earn around twice as much as what the average American household is going to make in a year.

Highly sought after

Employers are wanting people who know SQL! The more knowledge that you have about SQL the more sought after you are going to by employers. Knowing SQL is not only going to benefit you but your employer as well because they are not going to have to pay for you to learn the program. The interviewing process is going to be better than any other process that you have gone through and you may find that they are going to be willing to give you more money just for knowing SQL over the other person. With SQL knowledge, you are going to be opening yourself up for more careers than you might have been able to apply for before.

Get answers

SQL is going to give you the answers that you are looking for to any questions that you may have about business or data that is being stored inside of your data base. Therefore, you are going to be more self-sufficient and not as dependent on others when it comes to business. If you are able to answer questions on your own that you so that you are not stopping someone else from doing their job, then an employer is going to be able to save money by hiring you because you are going to be able to answer questions on hiring someone else to answer those questions. Knowing SQL is going to even help you if you are wanting to start your own business or push your business that you have already started to the next step that has just been out of your reach.

More stable than Excel

When you are using Excel for large amounts of data, you may notice that it is too much for the program and therefore the program tends to crash. A crash leads to lost data and extra time that you are going to have to go in and fix anything that may be wrong or entering data that was not saved. SQL is going to be much more reliable for you to use when you are trying to work with large amounts of data and it is going to save you some time working with it because it is not going to require too much for you to work with the processes that SQL offers.

Making reports

Searching in SQL is relatively easy and you can reuse that search when you have to double check to make sure that the data in the data base is accurate. Excel does not give you the proper processes that you need to get ahold of the data that you are wanting to get ahold of.

SQL coding only has to be written once and saved and then it is going to run each time that you need it to. This is yet another way that SQL makes it to where your life is easier because you are not having to take up as much time trying to get the data that you need.

Do not think that SQL is going to be simple, it is complicated and is going to take a lot of time to learn, but the more effort that you put into it, the more it is going to pay off for you. You are going to not only be saving money by learning SQL, but you are going to be increasing what you will be able to make with SQL.

## Four Tips That Make Using SQL Easier!

1. Changing the language on the user interface: close out the program if you have it open and then go to the installation folder. You will right click on the short cut that is on your desk top and open the file location. From there you will open the SQL developer folder and then the first folder that is listed will need to be opened nexted. The next thing that you are going to click on is the SQL developer.conf. You are going to be adding in a new setting inside of the text that is already there to change the language to what it is that you are wanting to see. You can put this new setting anywhere. Putting a comment in the code is going to be a good idea so that you know what you have done if you have to get back into it at a later date. You will AddVMOption before adding in the Duser.lanaguage and you can set it to any language that you are wanting. Now reopen your SQL developer and it will be in the language that you want it in.

2. Constructdata base connections: right click on the connection on the left of the screen and click on new connection. You will need to title the connection whatever it is that you want. You will need to enter the usertitle and password for it. You should change the color if you are going to be working with multiple connections at once. In the role you are going to change the role if you are using a system connection title. You can leave the home host alone if you are using your

home computer. However, if you are using a different location, you will need to input the IP address for where the system is going to be running. Leave your part alone and xe should be left alone as well unless you are not working with an express edition of SQL. You can test the connection and if it is successful, you can close the connection down and you have created your connection. If everything is correct it is going to open with no errors and you are going to be able to put in SQL code.

3. Disabling features: there are a lot of features that SQL offers and if you do not use them, then you should disable them so that they are not slowing down the developer. You will go to the tools menu and go down to the features option. Each feature has different folders, it is up to you to decide which features you want to keep running and which ones you want to disable. You can expand each folder down so that you are able to see what each folder contains. All you are going to do is uncheck the feature and it will turn that feature off and cause the system to start to run faster. Be sure that you are going to apply the changes so that they are not turning themselves back on without you turning them on yourself.

4. Executing commands and scripts: use the tool bar that is at the top of the developer and press the play button. Make sure that you have added in your semi colon. You can also use ctrl and enter so that you are not having to pull your hand off the keyboard. To run a script, you are going to you can use the toolbar again just select run scrpts so you run both commands. Or, press the F5 key if that is easier for you. Should your file be external use the at sign and the path file to import it and run it.

# Chapter 14. Workbook

This guidebook has taken a lot of time to look over many different topics when it comes to SQL, such as which data types you should use to work with your database in SQL. We even spent some time looking at the various commands that you would be able to choose when you are in SQL so you can initiate queries and search around inside the database.

Now that you have some of these basics down, it is time to move on to learn about the steps that you should take when you want to manage the objectivity that comes in the database. There are many things that we would be able to touch upon with regards to this in the guidebook, but some of the ones that we will spend our time on include tables, views, clusters, sequences, and synonyms. Let's start looking at these right now to help you understand how all of them will work in your code.

## What is the schema?

When you are working with what is known as a 'schema' inside of SQL, you should always think of it as using a set of objects that are already found inside of the database, but which will be linked to just one user on the database, rather than being linked to all of the users. The user who has the access will be the one who is the owner of the schema, and they will be the ones you can set the objects. These objects will then be linked directly back to the username that the owner picked. The user will have the power to generate their objects, and then when this is done, they can generate their own schema. This allows the user to have a ton of control over what is found in their databases and they could have the control to change it as much as they want.

You will find that this can be helpful in several ways. Let's say that your users just want to place an order with you. If they have their own account and schema, they would be able to make an order, and then they would be able to change or delete that order if they so choose.

Another example of this is when the user is trying to set up their own account in your store. This is something that they can sign up for and then they will have an account for your store. This is something that they can choose to do, and then they will go through and pick out the username and the password that they would like to use.

After the user has been able to set up their own account, they will have access to all parts of the database that pertain to them. They can make changes as well, such as updating their address, changing their payment options, and even making changes to the orders that they placed. In addition, any time that the user would like to be able to get into their account, all they need to do is use the username and password that they picked the first time and log in to mess around on the database.

Let's take a better look at how this will work by bringing out an example. Let's say that you are the person who has the credentials that are needed to log in. For this example, we will use the username 'PERSON1.' You can decide what you would like to place inside this database and you can even create a brand new table, for this one we will call it 'EMPLOYEES_TBL.' When you then go into the records, you will notice that for this new table, it will be called PERSON1 EMPLOYEES_TBL. This is how others will see the table name as well so they know who created the table. The schema will be the same for each person who created this table and owns it.

When you or your user would like to access their own schema, one that is prepared already, you will not have to list out the exact name of the schema. Instead, you would simply need to pull up the name that you gave it. So, for the example that we went through before, you would be able to call up EMPLOYEES_TBL. Remember that this is just with schemas that are in your own account. If you would like to be able to pull up schemas that are present somewhere else, you must add the username ahead of it.

## How to create a new table

There are many times when you are creating something new in a database, and you will need to bring out a table. These tables are nice because they can store and present the information that you would want to use. You will find that SQL makes it easy to create tables, and you will then be able to add information as needed. Whenever you want to create a new table, you just have to use the simple command of 'CREATE TABLE.' This command will allow you to bring up the table and start using it, but if you would like to fill it in and make the table look a certain way, there will be a few more steps that you will need to accomplish.

It is important to think about what you would like to have in the table, how you would like the table to look, how big it should be, and other information about the table to ensure that it is made properly. Almost all of the versions of SQL will provide you with characters that will make it easy to submit or terminate a statement to the server. With ORACLE, the semicolon will be the option that you would use, but with the Transact-SQL version, it is better to work with the GO command. But for most of these versions, you would be able to use the CREATE TABLE command and then when you are ready, you can start filling them out.

## How to create a table with one that already exists

There will be times that when you are working with SQL where you will want to take the information that you have from one table and then use that information to create a new table. This is something that you can do with SQL, you just need to learn the right commands to make sure that it works right. The commands that work the best for making this happen include the 'CREATE TABLE' and the 'SELECT' commands. Once you have been able to use these two commands, you will see that it worked to create a new table that will have the same parameters and definitions as your older table. This would like to create a new table that you can customize, but it would have the information that you need from an older table.

There is a little bit of coding to make all of this work for your needs. If you would like to take one of your older tables and use it as the basis of your new table, you would be able to use the following syntax:

CREATE TABLE NEW_TABLE_NAME AS

SELECT [ "|COLUMN1, COLUMN2]

FROM TABLE_NAME

[ WHERE];

As you take a look at this syntax, you should be able to see that the new syntax will use the keyword SELECT. This is the right keyword to use here because it is something that you can bring out any time that you would like to work on a query for that particular database. This SELECT keyword will help you to work on your new table, even while you are creating it, with the help of your search results.

### How to drop tables

The next thing that we will work on doing with the SQL system is how to drop tables. If you use a new keyword, the keyword 'RESTRICT' and then you reference a particular table by using the view or the constraint that is set up, the command 'DROP' will be used, but it will give you a message alerting you that there is an error in the system. It is also possible to add in the 'CASCADE' command along with the DROP command. This will make sure that the DROP command will work properly and that all the views and the constraints that are inside of your table will be dropped. To ensure that all of this will work out well for you, you can use the following syntax to drop a new table:

DROP TABLE TABLE_NAME [ RESTRICT | CASCADE]

Any time that you are interested in dropping your new table inside of the SQL database, you should make sure that you are telling the program who is the owner of this new table that you are working on. This is not always necessary, but it is a good habit to get into. This will ensure that you do not drop the wrong table and it will often help to prevent loss of information inside of the table. If you have access to some of the other accounts inside of your database which is not your own, it is important that you check that you are working inside the account that you want so that you do not change the wrong things and have to fix that mess later on.

Since you will work with a lot of information and databases when you work with SQL, it makes sense that these tables are an important part of working inside the SQL system. These tables will help you to gather information and present it in a way that you are easily able to read. The tables will then be able to take the information, or perhaps the products that you would like to sell, and they can present them to you in a way that is easier for you to look through. Or, you can set up the table so that it is easier for the user to look at it when they are on your website. As you can see, creating these tables is not something that has to be too difficult to work with, but they will certainly help you to keep the information in your database as safe as possible.

# How to Do Your Own Search Results Through SQL

As we have gone through this guidebook, we have spent a lot of time talking about search results and how SQL can help out with this. You can use SQL to make it easier for you and for your users to search for terms or items and have the right things show up. This is a great way to sort through all the information that is inside of the database, so you can organize it the right way and ensure that you are getting the right things.

Once you have set up your own database for your business, and you have taken the time to learn how to create some of your own tables, it is now time to learn how to do various search queries on this system. You can make the SQL language work for you to ensure that you can find any result that you would like as long as that information is found in the database. You do need to make sure that you have set up the database in the proper way so that your search will find the right information without encountering any kind of issue.

A good way to think about it is that there are times when people will come to visit your website, and they are there because they are looking for some particular product that you are trying to sell. Are you more interested in working with a database that is slow and brings back the wrong results for your user? No, this will make the user mad, and they will go and use a different store for their needs. It is much better to go with a database that is set up right so that it is fast and will return the results that are needed.

## How to create a new query

The first thing that we need to take a look at is how to create a new query. Before you even start this process, just keep in mind you are basically sending out information to the database that you already set up. Make sure that you are using the right command, which in this case will be the SELECT command so that you can send out the query that you are planning to use.

One example that you can look at for this is when you are working with a table that is responsible for holding onto all of the products that are in your database. To do this, you would just use your SELECT command to find out which products are on that table. Your user will then be able to type in the specific products that they are interested in finding, such as your best-selling items, ones that fit a certain price point, size, color, or brand, and so on. You will also be able to use any type of query that you want to make sure that the user can get the product that they want out of your database if it is there.

## How to work with the SELECT command

Any time that you are on your website, or you would like to create a new query inside of your database, you will also be able to use the SELECT command to make this happen. This command can take over the tasks of starting and executing the queries that you are trying to send out to the database and in most cases, you will simply need to add something into the statement rather than sending out the SELECT command. You can add anything that you would like such as the brand of the item and more before using the command.

Whenever you are ready to work with the SELECT command while working with SQL, there will be four main keywords that you will need to watch out for. Remember that these are commonly known as the four clauses. These clauses are listed below:

**SELECT**

This command must be combined with the 'FROM' command to obtain the necessary data in a format that is readable and organized. You will use this to help determine the data that will show up. The

SELECT clause will introduce the columns that you would like to see out of the search results, and then you can use the FROM to find the exact point that you need.

**FROM**

The SELECT and the FROM commands often go together. It is mandatory because it takes your search from everything in the database, down to just the things that you would like. You will need to have at least one FROM clause for this to work. A good example of a syntax that would use both the SELECT and the FROM properly are these:

SELEC [ * | ALL | DISTINCT COLUMN1, COLUMN2 ]

FROM TABLE1 [ , TABLE2];

**WHERE**

This is what you will use when there are multiple conditions within the clause. For example, it is the element in the query that will display the selective data after the user puts in the information that they want to find. If you are using this feature, the right conditions to have along with it are the 'AND' and 'OR' operators. The syntax that you should use for the WHERE command is this:

SELEC [ * | ALL | DISTINCT COLUMN1, COLUMN2 ]

FROM TABLE1 [ , TABLE2];

WHERE [ CONDITION1 | EXPRESSION 1 ]

[ AND CONDITION2 | EXPRESSION 2 ]

ORDER BY

You can use this clause to arrange the output of your query. The server can decide the order and the format that the different information comes up for the user after they do their basic query. The default for this query will be organizing the output going from A to Z, but you can make changes that you would like. The syntax that you can use for this will be the same as the one above, but add in the following line at the end:

ORDER BY COLUMN 1 | INTEGER [ ASC/DESC ]

All of these will need to be in place if you would like to see the SELECT command working properly and pulling out the right information that you are searching for with your query into the database.

## How does case sensitivity work?

As you are doing things inside your SQL database, you will not need to worry so much about the case sensitivity that you put in as you would with some of the other coding languages that you may have used in the past. You can work with both the upper case and the lower case letters that you would like, and they will work the same when you do your own searches. You even have the choice to look for the clauses and the statements and see how those will show up in your code.

Now that we have said this, there will be some times when this case sensitivity is really important. For example, let's say you're in a situation where you are working with objects of data. For the most part, that data that you will use will be written in upper case letters. The reason for this is because it will let other users see that something is consistent with the code and they will know why. It makes the code look better and makes much more sense as well.

Without this rule with the upper case, you would end up with one user typing in 'JOHN', and the other user will go with John and still, another user may go with john. A beginner who goes through the SQL language may be wondering if these mean the same things or not, and this can get confusing. It is better to have everything in upper case so that it matches and some issues with writing this code will be avoided.

Those who work with the SQL language agreed that using an upper case format was the best idea for avoiding this confusion because these are easier to read, and it matches up with what you may have done in some other databases that you worked with. If you are not using this upper case format when you are writing things out, you need to at least go with another method that will keep your titles consistent with what you are doing. If you write out all the names with the format of 'Name,' then this is the way that you will do it with all of them.

There are also many times when you will work with transactions in your database as well as the queries that we talked about earlier, and sometimes these will go together. These transactions are really important, although you may feel that this is some unimportant information that the user is not going to care all that much about. But if you don't use case sensitivity the right way, or make sure that the table is set up the way that it should be, you will end up with the wrong results showing up and everyone getting frustrated. No one wants to type words into a query and find out the results that keep coming up have nothing to do with what they want.

When you are creating a new database and working inside of it, you must make sure that the query is set up well. This will make it easier for your user to find the products and other items that they are looking for. No user wants to come onto your page and run into issues with finding the information that they need. When the user types in the keyword, they want to be able to get the right information.

Imagine how well it would go if the user was on your website and typed in the keywords for what they are looking for, and then the wrong product came up? Let's say that they went on and started looking for some new boots. If they typed that in and started getting results for kids' toys, they probably would be really mad at it. Most people would not even try it a second time and would leave the page to try some other site, leaving you without the sale.

Working with the right queries and making sure that they work the right way with your database is so critical so that the above scenario does not happen. You want to make sure that when the user types in a keyword that they want to use, they can get the items that match with what they are searching for. These queries can make sure that you can keep the customer happy, and it will avoid a ton of frustrations that will come from not being able to find what they want on your website.

Even if this is the way that you would like to use the database, there will still be times that you would want to make sure that there is a good search function for your user. If the user wants to be able to look through the database and find specific information, such as their account, information on which payment method they have available, or what kind of services you can provide, you will still want to make sure that you have the transactions set up so that it goes smoothly. Working to make sure that the database is set up well so you and the user can find what they want when they do a query in the search bar will ensure that the user is happy and that your business can run smoothly.

As a beginner, it is important that you learn how to set up the right queries that can be used inside of your database. This is important to help organize your SQL database and make sure the user finds what they're looking for. This is important whether you are trying to sell products on your website, whether you want to keep track of payment, and other personal information for the customer or you want to use the database for another reason. Make sure to use some of the steps that we outlined earlier in this chapter to help you set up the database in a manner that makes a lot of sense based on what your users need and will provide the right information as soon as a customer does a search on your database.

# Chapter 15. SQL Quiz

1. Transcribe SQL.

2. What is the keyword in creating tables?

3. What is the SQL syntax in selecting tables?

4. What is the keyword in deleting tables?

5. What is the SQL statement if you want to display only the names and the city of the table above?

6. What is the SQL statement if you want to retrieve only the data of employees who are 25 years old and above?

7. What is the SQL command if you want to arrange the names in an ascending order?

8. What is the SQL query if you want to fetch the data of employees, who have a salary of more than 20000.00?

9. What is the SQL command if you want to select only the employees coming from Denver?

10. What is the SQL if you want to change the Name of Lambert Jancy to Walker Jean?

**ANSWERS:**

1. STRUCTURED QUERY LANGUAGE

2. CREATE TABLE

3. SELECT "column_name1", "column_name2 FROM "table_name";

(Remember to remove the double quotes when substituting the names of your columns and tables.)

4. DELETE TABLE

5. SELECT Names, City FROM EmployeesSalary;

6. SELECT * FROM EmployeesSalary
WHERE Age >= 25;

7. SELECT * FROM EmployeesSalary
ORDER BY Names ASC;

8. SELECT * FROM EmployeesSalary
WHERE Salary >20000;

9. SELECT * FROM EmployeesSalary
WHERE City = 'Denver';

10. UPDATE EmployeesSalary
SET Names = 'Walker Jean'
WHERE Names = 'Lambert Jancy';

# CONCLUSION

For a long time now, data analysis has always been done as a part of business. The business intelligence team has always been the part of business that has been mandated with information retrieval as well as pulling down databases and relying information to other parts of business through the local machines. This has changed so much with the advancement of computer technology.

All businesses are now into digital businesses. Everyone is in the data business and so some of the important skills have to be mastered in order to make things easy to run such businesses. Every day, new data is created for a business and by the time you realize it, a business has produced and consumed digital data. This is the point where the querying and analysis of digital quantitative data becomes an important skill that everyone must learn.

SQL is like an emerging new skill that is quite vital to businesses. Just like basic literacy is important for any job out there, mastery of SQL skills is increasingly becoming important for anyone that wants to succeed in the business sector.

You realize that if everyone you work with is data literate, working can be very easy since everyone can create, access and manipulate data in the databases and perform all the required tasks without waiting for the other.